Hidden Places & Hidden Faces

A Southern Anthology

Skull Hunny Review

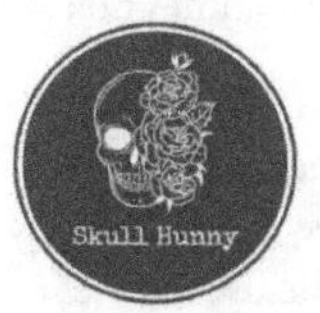

Cover Photography by Carl Scharwath

Cover Design by Cynthia Schaefer

*Full page images by Eliana Vanessa

This is Skull Hunny's debut anthology of southern poets and artists.

Skull Hunny accepts submissions of poetry and black and white artwork or photography. All submissions must include 65 word bio with headshot. Please format submissions in a word document with one titled work per page in Roman Numeral font, size 12, double spaced. Refer to www.elianavanessa.com for submission dates and details. Although reasonable care is taken, Skull Honey assumes no responsibility for the loss of unsolicited material.

With gratitude to God, without which none of this would be possible, my spirits, and, of course friends & family who believe in me & who looked over the early drafts of this edition.

To all the artists and their relentless dedication to this project. Thank U. Without your encouragement, I might have given up — and we would have missed out on this fun!

Introducing Special Guest Poet :

Isabella R. Smith

Contents

Susan S. Newton

Tobi Alfier

William R. Gallaher

Valentine Pierce

Kendall Elizabeth Smith & Isabella MacDonald Smith

Dennis Formento

Cynthia Schaefer

Eliana Vanessa

Three Photographers

Gerardo Aristimuno

Susan S. Newton

Autumnal Splendor

Driving that Louisiana country road
in old pickup truck,
headed for supplies in town

Main thing visible is
brilliant orange and gold,
fading into the blueness of sky

Towering trees, filled with
color ready to burst;
know it won't be long

Bridges and streams we pass,
farms, livestock, fields,
more old trucks

All the while,
the steady beat of falling foliage
hums its own kind of lullaby

These beautiful leaves,
ready to surrender into the earth,
relay the greatest show autumn offers

Miles and more, and more
serenity, fragility, hope
we see, we feel

Finally, home again, barn, dogs, family
our lovely ride in the country is
done....for now.

Brown Water

Brown Water is the only kind I know.

From our rivers to our bayous,
it's my roots - my Louisiana background.
It's where I grew up and thrived.

Brown water is memories of fishing with daddy,
of tubing on the Tickfaw River with friends,
of splashing around off Ponchatoula Beach.

Brown water was catching crabs in the bayou,
and swimming at Grand Isle
with my younger brother.

Yes, clear water is pretty and inviting,
but only brown water is dense enough
to hold all MY memories.

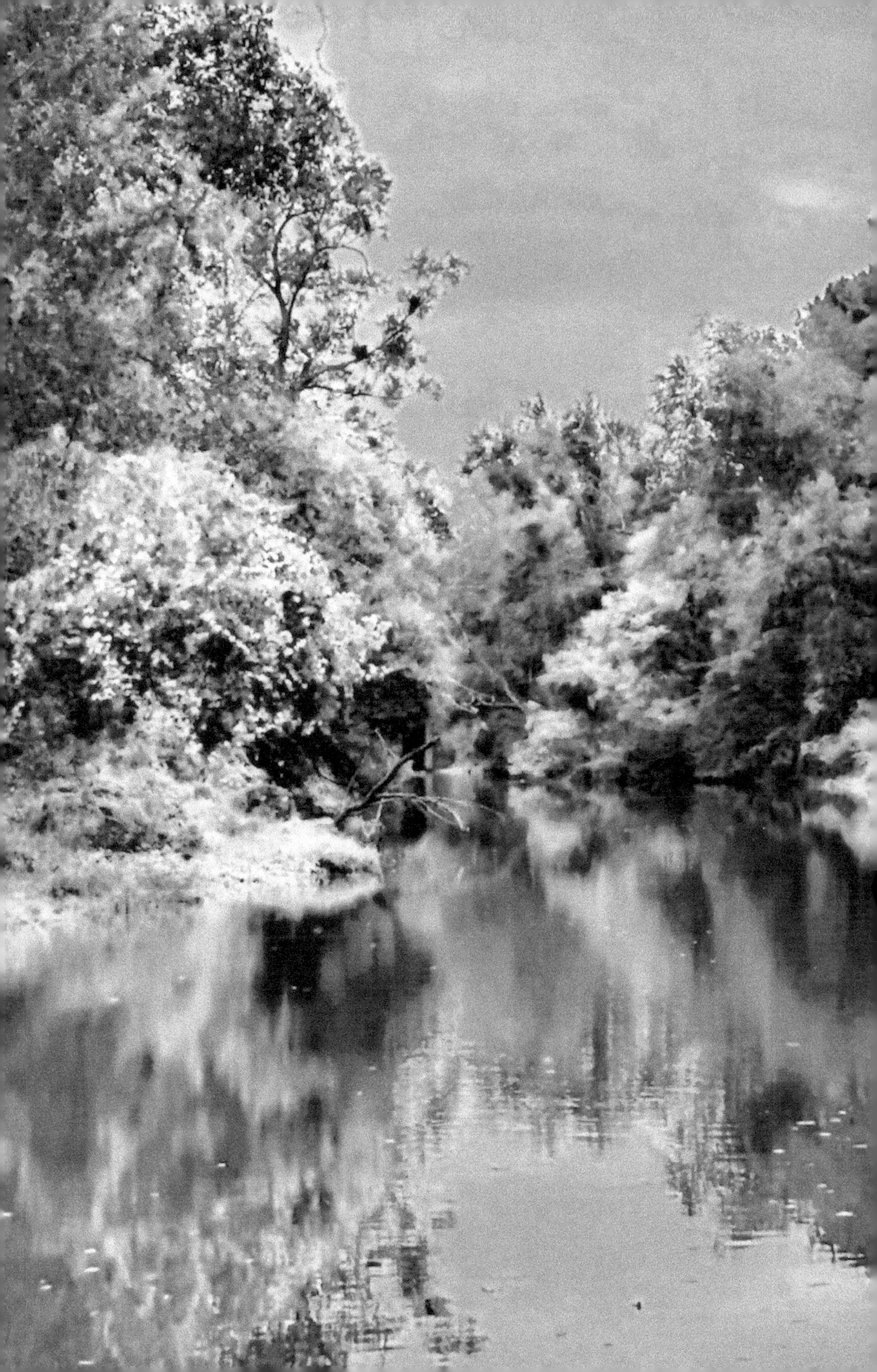

Breakfast on the Balcony

73 delightful degrees this Covington morn –
perfect for breakfast on the balcony!

Sun low on horizon
peeps around willow tree.

Sky soft blue,
rising from whiteness of sunrise.

Wisps of clouds float by
ever so slow-ly.

Pond sits still, aptly
reflecting its surroundings.

Birds chirp as they rest on limbs,
casting the calls of a new day.

How nice to wake up with nature!

All form part of a rhythmic, morning symphony,
Of which I am but a single string!

Sunrise

Sleepy eyes barely behold
the waking of the Earth.

Eastern view of the North Shore
beholds a brand-new day,

A new promise offering,
more than the day before.

Renewed spirit, rekindled flame,
poised to do it all over again.

Heavy hearts and broken souls,
can't resist the assurance of sunrise.

We take that pledge with us
through the balance of the day,

Searching for the fulfillment
of the pledge.

Sunset

The heavens are ablaze tonight,
in a radiant kaleidoscope -

last dying embers so stunning,
rapidly fading into horizontal oblivion.

I gaze out of my evening window
in absolute, awestruck gratitude!

What a gift sunset is –
a true statement of our magnificent planet.

And when seen from the Causeway Bridge,
one feels totally unlimited by time.

We are here but a short time,
in immense scale of eons of existence.

Yet, we are recipients of grandeur
greater than our own awareness.

Sunset – one small expression
of the hope we have for the future –

the hope we need to carry on.

Tobi Alfier

Man as Broken Levee

Stars tattooed over
the scar on his neck,
phoenix wrapped around
his broken femur.
Lord, this body has
so many stories…
    Like a breached levee.
Trash flooding downstream
leaving in its wake:
ruined houses, wrecked
opportunities
for a life that's good,
with love and laughter,
the same fine woman
for more than a month.
He is an honest
man, just loves his drink.
Ain't no place for booze
with a missus who
craves a family.
You can't be a dad
if you ain't at home,
your place at the bar
isn't the dinner
table. What is right…
    Twenty feet of mud
wrecking a stunning
house, with two babies
bawlin' and the wash
pinned up in the sun,
or an ice cold brew,
a catch of seabass,
buddies with nicknames
you can't even say.

You gotta decide
on priorities
before that levee
bursts, and once again
you ain't got nothin'
but a cloud of stars,
stories to keep warm
with on winter nights,
no woman, no kids,
no plans, no nuthin'.

Heading Home

LaLa Cherie lived in a dump
of an apartment on a side street
in the French Quarter. Her granny,
mum, and the odd cousin or three
had air mattresses and got eyes-up close
with an occasional cockroach or mouse,
nothing they ain't seen before.

LaLa got teased bigtime in school,
her drag name fighting like hell
with straight A's, participation in every club
you could conjure, and a place on the special
student/faculty board to help solve problems
and keep every drug from mouth or vein. Too many kids
had died, and a teacher or two, it wasn't right.

When granny passed, LaLa kept it so far inside
no one would ever know and she'd never tell.
She passed by Marie Laveau's heading home
from school, bought some safe-travel stones
to string upon her neck and that was that.
She rolled up her cuffs, waded into the Mississippi
far down from the docks, blessed the old woman

ten times by always, then came home
to help with supper. LaLa made cornbread.
Mum made red beans and rice.
They threw in a ham hock in honor of gran,
keeper of the budget and all things costing
a dollar or more. A couple extra cousins came,
gran's place at the table stayed set and bare,

and the late sun sank hard into dusk.

Carmen Walks the Camino de Santiago

Monday through Saturday Carmen
watches out her window, mother-of-pearl
cleavage at rest on the peeling husk of the frame.
A small gold cross, and smaller earrings

complete a pastoral still-life
against the faint piss-smell and detritus
of an alley off Bourbon Street
known for its women of all hours.

If her window is closed, she is busy.
If her window is closed, it is Sunday,
a day for Vieux Carre Baptist Church—
where they know she is broken

but do not care. Carmen keeps two
cigar boxes from her beloved grandfather
in which to save money—
one for Sundays, one for her dream

to walk the Camino, to walk with undiluted faith,
trek with the other pilgrims, all damaged
in some way, all searching for blessing, sense
of connection, some way out of unspoken grief.

Carmen counted the bunched-up bills in that box
like a child counts the hours until bedtime.
She stopped one day after church, took a modest
passport photo, and bought her ticket to all the hopes

her years amounted to. She paid her rent,
latched her window for at least two months,
and began her journey the way a blind woman
remembers the way through her house.

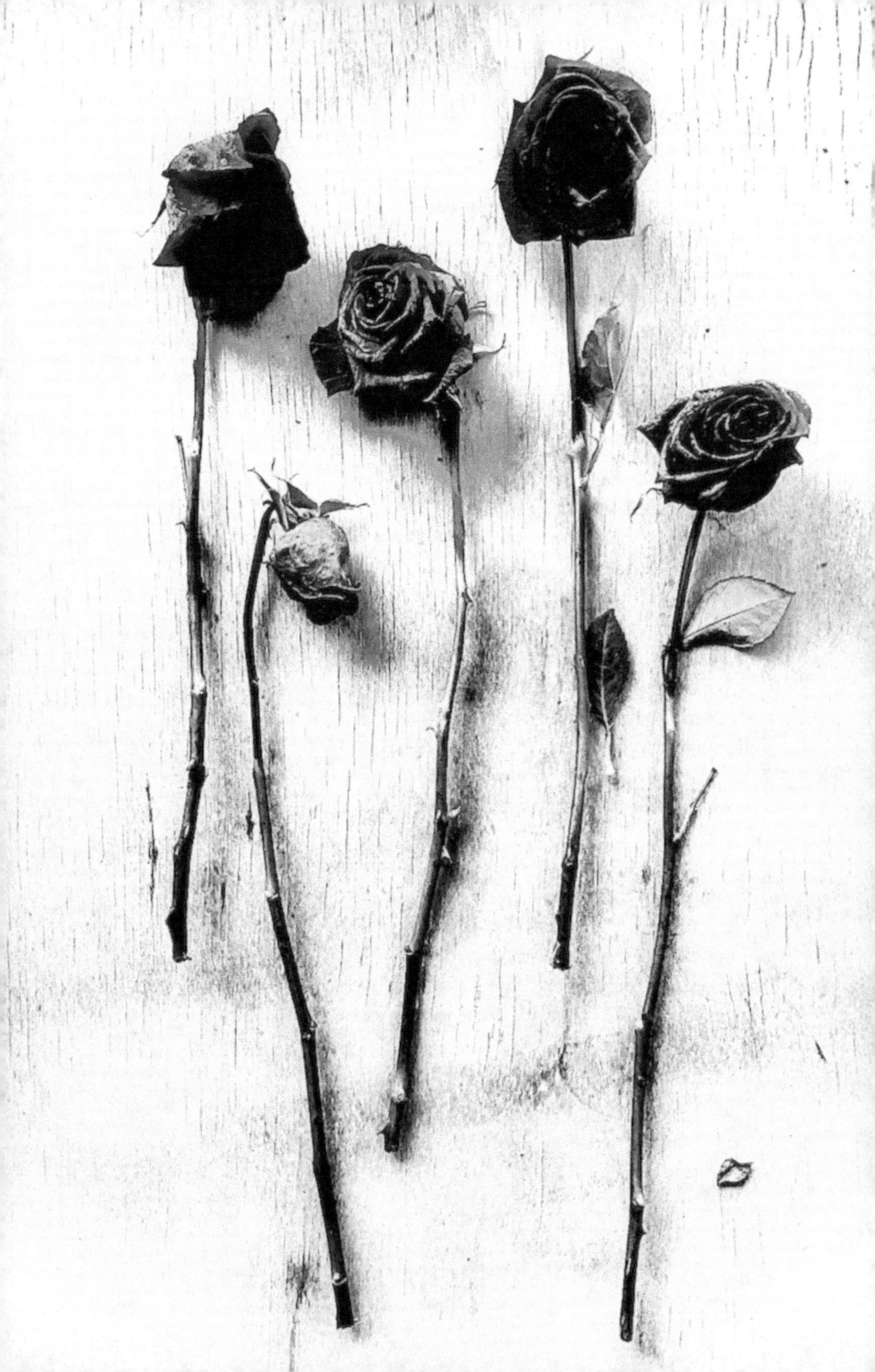

Bourbon Street Angels

I hear angels hang out on Bourbon St.
They survey their territory,
stomp old stomping grounds,
elbow each other when some drunk
drifts out of Lafitte's to his car.

They do not guide or save anyone,
they just survey
the doings of folks with a dollar or two
craving booze-lit zydeco,
prize any soul who drops change
in the cup of some poor boy tap-dancing
on the street to help his mama make rent.

Come first light, they pretend to have breakfast,
knock powdered sugar off each other
while they watch the couples
stopping for coffee and beignets
after a few hours between the sheets.
They know there is nothing like the taste
of sugar after the taste of sex.

They call each other *cher* but don't speak
French, don't speak to anyone but themselves.
No one can see them, that's how they want it.
They look perfect, undiminished,
but only to each other. They never have to face
mirrors, their stories told, silenced long ago.

William R. Gallaher

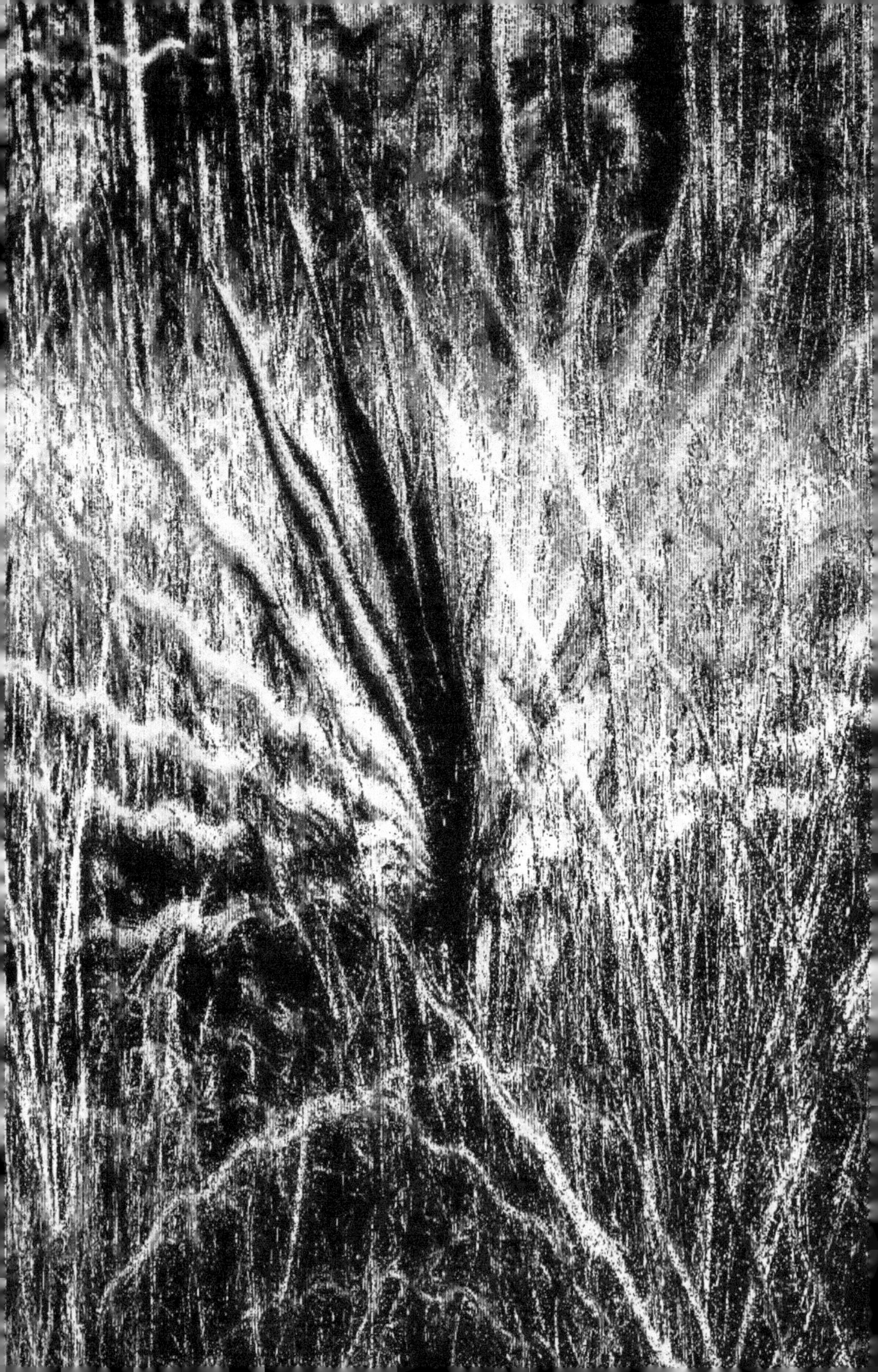

A Tavern

All about New Orleans
Taverns of a curtain age
Evoking this place of ancient aura
A lady who knows who she is
Has ever been and always will be,
A really live oak adorned by lace
Of Spanish moss in moonlight.

So also the tavern
Enveloping arms of warm woods
The best and most durable
The mahogany, the cherry, the oak,
The cypress one with the wetland.
A perfect backdrop for one who thirsts.

Coming in for a cold one,
Or sanctuary from the day or week,
Or human companionship,
Of any of many sorts
From the endless human menu.

The buddies to watch the game,
The besties to comfort heartbreak,
The other couples with kids,
Who need friends for a night on the town.
And the anxiously seeking single,
In search of someone new,
Or the patiently listening barkeep,
Eyes on swivels, ears attentive
Amid tending to other patrons,

The din of human decibels
Rises muddled absorbed by carved ceiling
Mixing in muffled echoes

That swallow up softspoken secrets.

The filtering reflection in backbar mirrors,
The light never too little or too much,
Somehow softening features to look better than you are.

Not at all like a church of marble,
That may be sculpted, but unchanged.
Wood still exudes the life it had,
And only preserved, carved and stained,
Becoming, like the patrons it embraces,
Something slightly molded,
By libation and conversation,
Into what they aspire to be.
In ordering a quick refresher,
Or staying for hours on end.

French doors open to the world
Admitting a freshening breeze
Wafting in sights and sounds, and fragrance,
An old tavern where cares are forgotten,
In an enduring human cradle that feels home.

An Elderly Reverie

Sitting on a rocker on her wide front porch,
With a view of the lake and the live oaks beside it,
The elderly woman sat patiently, waiting for her son to arrive.
Nearly 80 now, born, raised, educated and married in New Orleans,
She and her husband had built this Northshore haven,
Away from the hustle and bustle of the city,
But still very much in touch with its heart.

Frank had passed some time ago now, his heart too big for his health,
But she had her boys, and her daughter a nurse,
And he had well provided for her, both in life and after life.
She wiped a tear from each eye, and she shook
with how much he missed him.
But Danny, her eldest, was coming by, and bringing the grandkids,
And they would all delight in devouring MawMaw's French toast.

As she rocked a bit more, a reminiscence took form,
Of the unforgettable morning Danny had been conceived.
They had debated the night before, was it a good time to try or not,
She smiled as she recalled they concluded it was less than ideal.
But in the morning, her answer had been quite different.

She had gotten up, put on the coffee, and returned to the bedroom.
She looked around the 4th floor attic walkup, as romantic as Paris,
Just four rooms, diminutive, but overlooking the roofs of the Quarter.
Mists were still dissipating in the early dawn,
floating across the rooftops,
Sunlight glinted off damp slate tiles, like twinkling lights in twilight.
The aroma of chicory coffee and her own fertile scents
mixed in harmony.

So she decided, right then and there, and threw off her nightgown,
Planting her bare legs astride her husband who roused quickly,

Her naked body on full display for his enjoyment,
Her nipples reaching out toward her lover,
Both hands gathering her hair above her head.
An irresistible force, glistening in morning light,
Not to be questioned, but simply embraced.

Unbridled passion, too often made tawdry, even holy this day,
Fully engaged with sacred purpose, open to new life.

Perspiring a bit now, even so many decades later,
She recalled rivulets of sweat down the small of her back,
Excitement making her skin tingle all over in ecstasy,
Thighs trembling with pleasure, welling from the depths of her soul.
The bells of the Angelis adding their vibrations to the bedroom,
An adjunct cathedral alive with love and hope for new life.
Guttural cries to heaven from her heaving chest.
Hanging on by her fingernails to the tensing shoulders of her man.

Then spent, and collapsing upon him,
holding him so the moment would not end.
Clinging to the dawn of a motherhood that would last forever.

The elderly lady took a deep breath, to recover from her reverie.
Her adult children would never imagine what old mothers remember.
Memories fade with age, but some are ingrained on the heart.
Danny came along nine months later, and was on his way again.
So she straightened herself up, tried to will the rose from her cheeks,
Lest he think she was somehow ill, and summon his sister
to tend to Mom.

Not long after, the car turned the corner
and made its way to the driveway.
Oh, how she wished her Frank could be here,
but then, as her son emerged,
She could see the strong resemblance,
and knew her Frank was here after all.
The grandkids ran up to her,

her son inhaled the chicory coffee,
and French toast was on.

A part of that tiny Quarter apartment was still with her across the lake,
In the life so well begun, by choice, that morning long ago.
She was all smiles.

Valentine Pierce

Just Tuesday

It's just Tuesday
everywhere else
a weekday
a work day
a worry day
but here
it is throw-your-cares-away day
throw-me-something-mister day
can-I-have-that-lady day
dance-in-the-street day
paint-your-face-and-body day
dress-fabulously-silly day

today is just Tuesday
everywhere else
but here it is Mardi Gras Day
Al "Carnival Time" Johnson day
because today in New Orleans
is the only day of its kind
in this country.

Today is Fat Tuesday
but tomorrow, tomorrow is still
Ash Wednesday

Backroads

I have no backroad stories,
No adventures in small towns,
No rural stops, no farm house dinners.
Folks love the back roads
I would love them too
If those odd turns didn't baffle me
If those changes in direction
Didn't cause me panic.

But I know better
My brain goes haywire
At the least little detour
It can't finds its way
It needs a paper map
A flashlight at night
A well-lit corner
To not lose my way altogether.

When they were young my children teased,
"Mom gets lost going in a straight line."
It's less true with GPS but if GPS fails
I'll have to send up flares.

In Memorium

I remember club sandwiches at Woolworth's lunch counter
The smell of fabric we bought at Krauss
Our Christmas pilgrimages to Canal Street
To see Mr. Bingle dance in D.H. Homes window.

It seems as if it was only days
After K&B finally came to our neighborhood
That they decide to sell every purple piece and pen.
We thought K&B was immortal right until they day
It metamorphosed into Rite Aid and ceased to exist.
D.H. Holmes lives on in Dillard but lacks its spirit.

Krauss' carcass stands as a crumbling monument
To the days the five & dimes,
To the stores where a few dollars
Could buy enough fabric to clothe eight children.
To this day I can't describe the smell of that fabric
But I would know it anywhere.
Krauss, gone only months after the king

Of the five & dime, F.W. Woolworth, was dethroned.
Woolworth's sold the popcorn Momma always brought home
With the shoes and fabric and school supplies. 15¢ a bag.
It's carcass stands, too, shouldered
By all the new-age dollar stores
And quick cash, payday broke places.
I miss these moments in my life.

There are things I miss more, though:
A body hidden behind a granite wall,
In a crypt, in Kenner, baby brother.
Urns stored away
In crypts in New Orleans, mother, sisters.

A casket in Texas, my girl child.
I would give up all the rest for these.

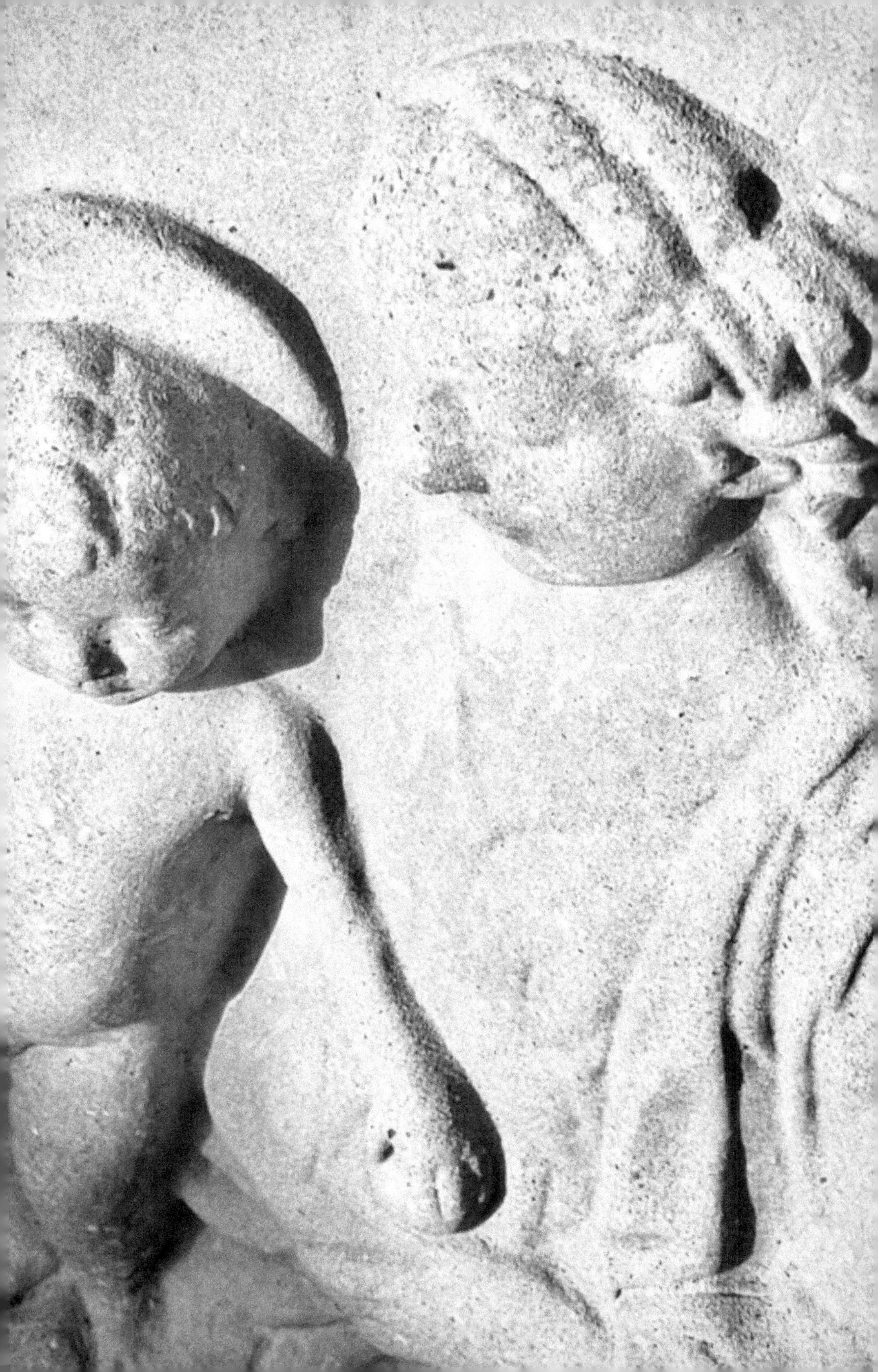

First Love

Phoenix woos me with dream-
Sweet skies as clear as music,
Days bright as heaven.
Almost wins my heart in the daylight,
But at night, encased in the cool,
Dry arms of the desert,
I pine for my first love, New Orleans.
She is the mother of my child-dreams.
I long to feel her hot summer rain kisses
Upon my cheek;
I crave her cotton-candy clouds,
Their sugary sweetness making me high;
I ache to see mosquito hawks,
Their gossamer wings so impossible
It hardly seems they can fly.
I want to fly, too, but I cannot in this desert heat.
Home, let me go home
To my goddess, queen, mother —
New Orleans, my first love.

Kendall Elizabeth Smith & Isabella MacDonald Smith

Regrets to the Egrets

Male and female egrets stand
Still as statues
Heads held at same level
Not touching

Necks extend
press forward
Eyes stare straight ahead
Not moving

Mesmerized
Inside their spirits
Invisible tears flow
Not seen

For thousands of years
Their instincts knew once the pond was there
This is where they rested
Among the rusted soda cans
Waving grass, crawfish
Not now

Their Meadowbrook pond disappeared
Their waving grass destroyed
Their food, their home
Not habitable

Widening the highway

Machines filled in their pond
Macadam hardened to encase theirspace
Not now their birthing place

Go to Greenleaves Kendall shouted
Don't get too close
Metal arms spray water
Whirring motor
Not safe

Greenleaves' Canadian geese
Peck and honk you to flight

Not welcomed

Regrets to the egrets as they soar aloft
Filling the sky
Joined by others who now have no home

Not your concern.

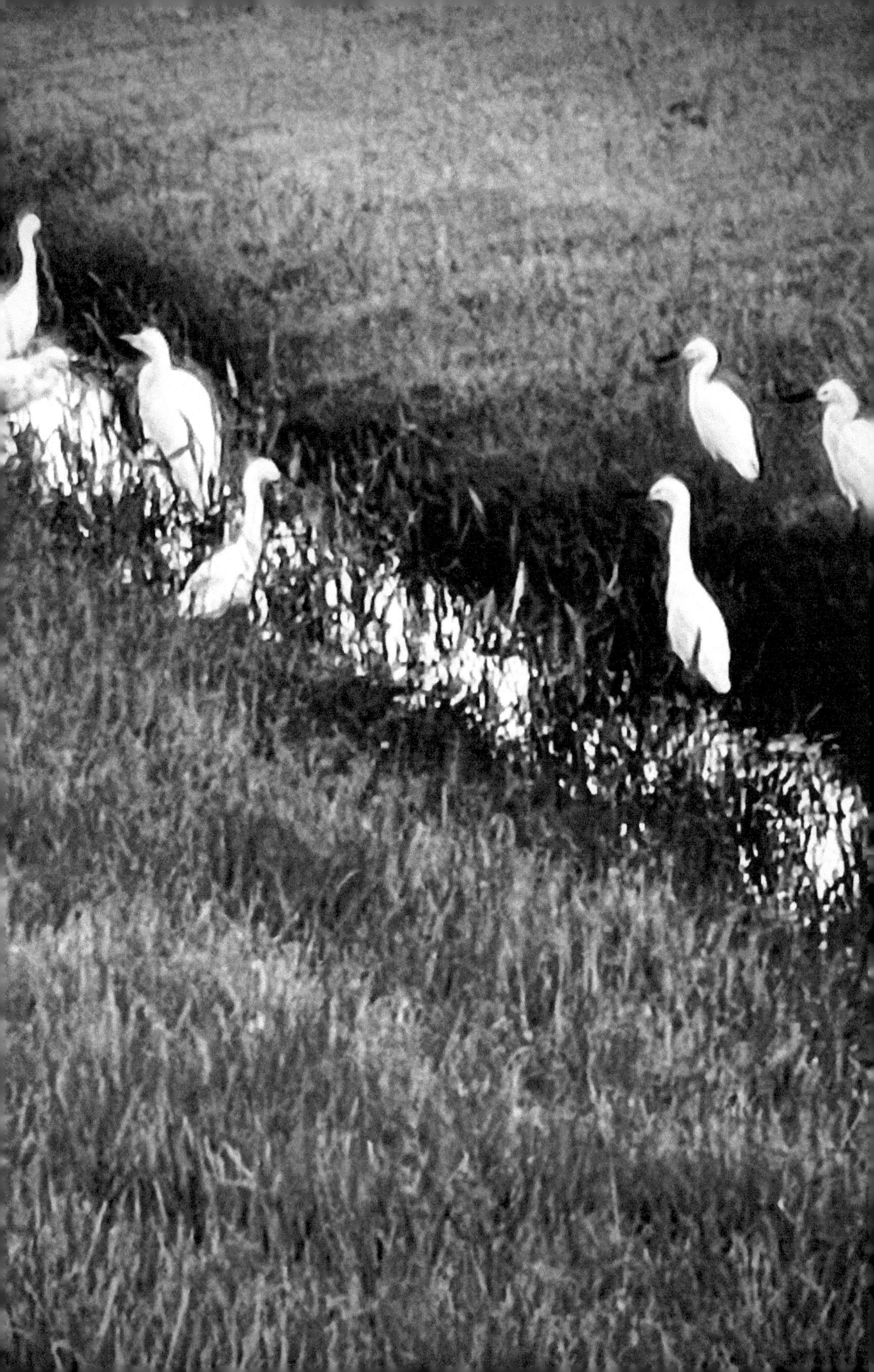

Dennis Formento

Habib

Habib true bearer of the Beat torch of travel and explorer of world soul.
El Habib whose name means "sweetheart"
you hear the world calling you
Habib, even in the boom-flash of a "just" war
someone must bear witness to the innumerable dead
the rapes, the animal deaths
rivers polluted by blood and chemical waste
blistered houses, undrinkable water of Flint
the old men who die in hospitals without power
Cold war bullets kill just as dead as ever a hot war did
if ever was a true cold war, with proxy wars aplenty
old women who drink tea in the shade of a tortured wall
cast shadows on the wall of a bus station in Portland, Habib,
where you traced the steps of Kerouac and Ginsberg
and a generation of hot cars
blasting through walls of segregated America
LeRoi Jones, Bob Kaufman
with "the unspeakable visions of the individual"
Cease and still be until the vision comes
El Habib, trapped, with no way out of town
give glory to the moon
Habib we should Skype soon
the voices of individuals invading cold rooms
Stasis is immobile, hostile forms
too solid to imprison you for long.

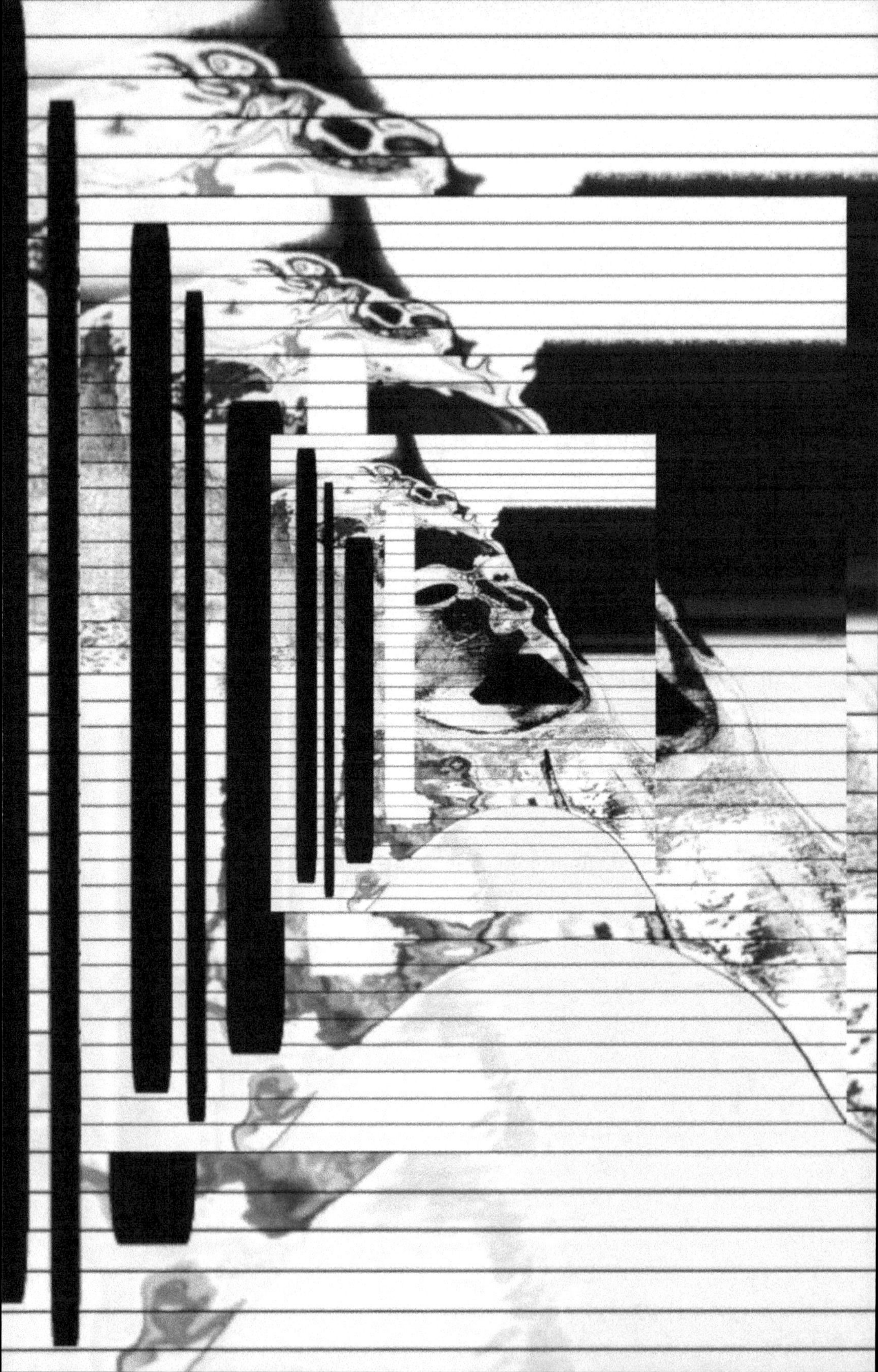

Coffee House Kisses

It isn't bad waking up to the sound of chirping birds and a beautiful lady pushing kisses on me with her caramel lips, teetering on her shoes in a waking dream of New Orleans coffee culture houses beginning with Robert Borsodi's where the tables bled honey-yellowed decoupage pictures of clowns from Fellini's *8 ½* and a live dove sailed loose over your head and remarkably no excrement on the tables; Bob doing his usual slow mo is better molasses in January delivery of a tuna melt known as a Rick Brown on a bagel with a cup of Joe or red-headed wide eyed Diane Carson's Until Waiting Fills in the late 70s on Chartres, and I danced with her once, she was light as heaven but ran away to Kansas with some guy from New Jersey, with a waitress on skates delivering coffee on a hot July day, and a young black man saying, "I like this place," tho clearly he was freaked out of his wits that anyone would buy him a coffee on such a hot day while waiting for a paycheck from the guy across the street and the Magic Bean Lady sticks her head in the door and makes funny signs in the air and mutters *cantabile*impreca-tions because no, you didn't need any magic beans today (you would have to carry them by hand to California and dip them in the ocean to make them work)

and no dreary-eyed punk from Cali can come here and accuse me of being some monster from America's past, some beatnik, some hippie, some old guy out for a lay (the same thing they used to beat Jack Kerouac to death, only now it's been perfected, they don't have to do it themselves after 30 years of punk)

where Fair Grinds holds its own giving away free coffee six months after the Apocalypse with a jar of dog biscuits on the stairway—first it was a biker bar, then True Brew, and poet Bill Myers lived above it, threw mighty poetry parties in his livingroom where you got water gunned if you went on too long, and the bathtub leaked into the coffeeshop downstairs where the granola was stale but I ate it anyway because the barista was cute, and now I'm marrying her and the owners chased all of the smokers out of the room, under the leaky balcony of Bill's apartment in time for the spring rains, lost $100 a day income and blamed the baristas, then fired them—

and once I tried out to be the radio voice of Andrei Codrescu, but they said I didn't look like him—Flora's held its own with poetry and drummers kept a steady polyrhythm, the fourteen ounce burritos are still only 4 bucks and every stick of furniture is lined with smoke—it survived miraculously the Third World War known as Katrina and Sound Café owned by pretty Baty, all gleaming and clean interiors, with its bookshop out back, jazz on Sundays, parklike somehow at the end of a rough urban street

and in 1994, the first peasant to throw coffee beans, Kaldi's on Friday night, jazz-poetry throwdowns and I talked for two hours with a beautiful anarchist about Mediterranean refrigerators & never saw her again, *Full Moon Night*, and a pitch-perfect blend of the bell of Coltrane's horn and a trumpet-moon—O – Nick Sanzenbach on keys, Mark Flower fowling the growling guitar, Arturo Pfister led the parade of poets or joined Sinclair, Dalilah played bongos, the portable back to Africa transmission—and according to the *Picayune*, "intellectuals" gathered there to match wits or play chess out of the broiling sun, & ten New Years of the Ten Thousand Croissants piled out of memory and I never will be mistaken for an old Spanish notebook, but I didn't just cook this up, I was there;

if you could drop a bomb on Rue de la Course you would kill half the Tulane law school

the eminent vulgarity of "a coffee house poet" rears its ugly head topped by a beanie—and always back to Robert Borsodi; so sweet you could drink him through a straw, sentimental poet, antibusinessman, who gave away everything for free because it was easier than counting money —and the lady who towered above me in the wee hours is gone, it is days later and I can still smell her lipstick

When I Chop Okra

I don't think about anything else
I don't lose my fear of the blade
Okra becomes sticky the instant I slice it
ropy is as ropy does
When I chop okra
I always want to save the tips
The tips and the tops look good in my compost
I do not chit or chat
When I chop okra
They are never the same size, the pieces
they look dry until you touch them
Two pieces never look the same
Two whole okra never look the same
and the curved ones are never curved in the same way
"Get bent" has never meant the same to me
And I've never known what it meant anyway
The more I chop okra
the more I smell ham, tomatoes
onions sauteeing in the pan
the more rice I smell
the more gumbo, the more jambalaya
the more eggs beaten and fried
for breakfast, with okra on the side
eaten for lunch with fish and another vegetable
sweet potato maybe
corn on the cob
quintessentially American
Indian African gombo
In Italy, okra is called "gombo"
And you can find some seeds if you look hard enough
and the post office is willing to deliver

Cynthia Schaefer

A Moment for Myself

From Mother Me: Poems for Moms with Toddlers

The day feels like a boat
splashing through the water
passing by the lakefront close,
but far enough from the
pier I could not touch it
as I reached out.
The cool air,
a burst from the freezer,
the waves sloshing up and down.
The wake from the boat is gone.
Moss flows and branches sway
in the wind off the lake as I watch
children play passing the football.
The temperature dip
has me back in my car
as I say goodbye.
I turn to see a man in a coat
sitting on the stairs of the pier,
arms outstretched, coat billowing
with the gust of the moment.

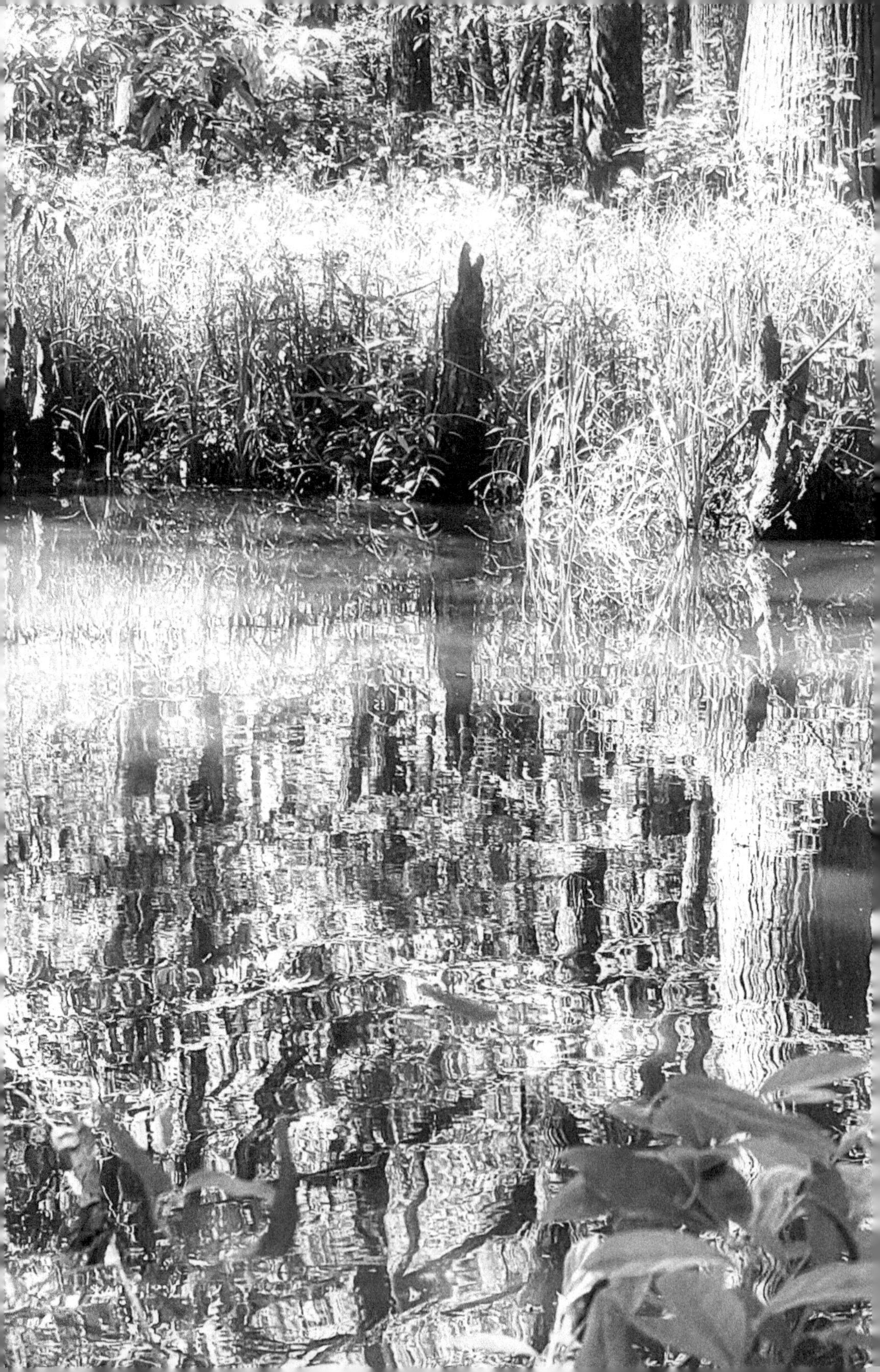

Marsh Grass

Let the boat fly through the water
kicking up a frothy white wake,
emanating to shores and marsh
where tall reeds rise
to catch a breeze and dance.
Roots green, tips tan from sun,
waves push against the clumps
of endless tall grass
that goes on for miles.

Walking in Abita – Part 1

I walk onto the trace in Abita Springs
past the brew pub on my left,
a Victorian white pavilion on my right,
where a bronze Choctaw Princess kneels
at a healing spring.
An anxious glance over my shoulder,
checking for a biker that is not there,
I exit down the steep sidewalk that empties
into an uninhabited splash pad,
dry in off-season hours left waiting for a summer day.
Past a sand filled wooden playground
surrounded by colorful child-painted murals
that fade on lopsided fencing
meant to keep in littles and sand, that too often stream out
in-between openings in the fence boards.
Past the two white sheltered structures
where desolate picnic tables rest,
till the sidewalk opens
in a vacant, vast round concrete amphitheater that lingers,
wondering when and who will gather there to entertain.

Walking in Abita – Part II

My feet carry me onto the wooden bridge
that crosses the Abita River flowing
like my thoughts, I wonder
what structure I can build to carry me
over them. The tree covered dirt trail
carves out in front of me,
the thick canopy overhead. I look up,
seeing the sunlight laugh at me
through glimpses in the leaves.
It oozes down hot amber, encasing me
in its light, burning my skin
like a mosquito trapped,
held in time for another age.
My beauty, my adulthood, sits hardening
until a child's hand grasps me in the gilded light of day
to pull me out of this daydream
where time does wane, and eyes lids grow heavy
with the thoughts that toil in spinning haze.
Tomorrows to-dos gunk
in a solid resin
that will not thaw
or burn away.

Dawn's Iris

From Mother Me: Poems for Moms with Toddlers

Enchanted with the morning sun
letting it surround me with love
knowing today can bring it's share of
anything and everything.
The kids can get sick.
The house can get messy.
The spouse can call upset.
A Louisiana Iris
emerging from damp soil,
roots spread, stalk bending
toward dawns beams,
budding through adversity
in purple, white and gold.
I can shine, I can move and I can grow
I can find new ways to hold on to myself
to be the one the children ask for:
I am worthy of every kiss and every hug
steady in self compassion
for I am blossoming.

Eliana Vanessa

another gum tree cut

this is
a cemetery,
and we shall
call it Love.
who has time, really,
for another poem?
relax—
for i am the tree,
the stump ,
and the axe;
a tourmaline grounded
in awareness,
bleeding,
from the roots, up.

wormwood

lichens ripen
beneath your
beating wings;
cherishing obscenities,
as wormwood,
and her frailties
trail frivolous things,
much like
the sting of a hornet's
kiss in the wind—
these shadow
offerings
weigh heavily
on the vine
as bruised bodies
conjure demons
to stumble and writhe;
a tune
of lost stares
now added
to the penalty,
no one said hatred would be easy.

grace of an angel

my love,
demon born
with a weapon
in his mouth;
shotgun pointed
tilted south,
bound to a lack
of logic found—
step away from the manger,
strangulate the stranger
who does not want
to recognize the danger;
a gravity
in dark eyes, censored,
rest assured
ten thousand apples
will fall in his favor,
bite with the grace
of an angel—-
swallow
the hallowed hollow,
if not for a sliver
of your sanity
tomorrow.

death at its best

the priest
summons
a ghost anew,
leaves of dew,
Nature's jewelry.

seven candles
lit from behind,
because
symmetry is blind;

drip of wax
and red wine
with which to bind
an unkindness
of ravens;

havens
that cannot
exist in solidarity,
such is the call
of spirituality;

will and bone, that fit,
exhuming
cannibalistic wit—
leaving Poetry
and Love,
now chafing at the bit.

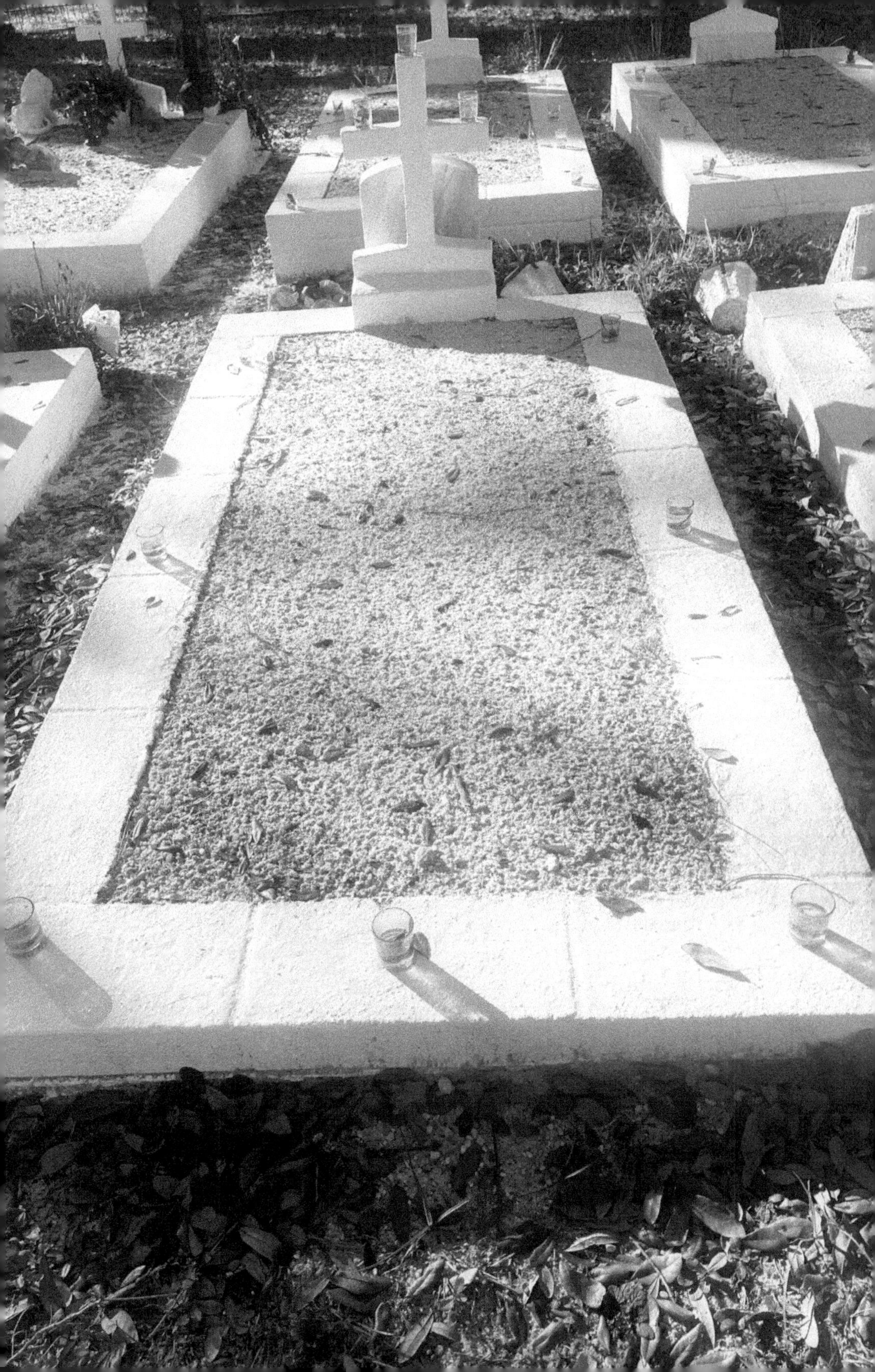

stealing songs

loved me so much
stole my pitiful words;

every ditty written
that boy had to hoard.

lordy, lordy
lordy, lord

bored, I was,
singing songs just because

what he don't know
won't kill him though;

those words
weren't mine—
evil crossing the mind;

vodou in time
cost the devil a dime,
the devil a dime
to rhythm and rhyme;

chants moving bodies down a second line;
me in my black dress...feeling just fine.

Three Photographers

Carl Scharwath

Ponce Inlet Lighthouse & Museum

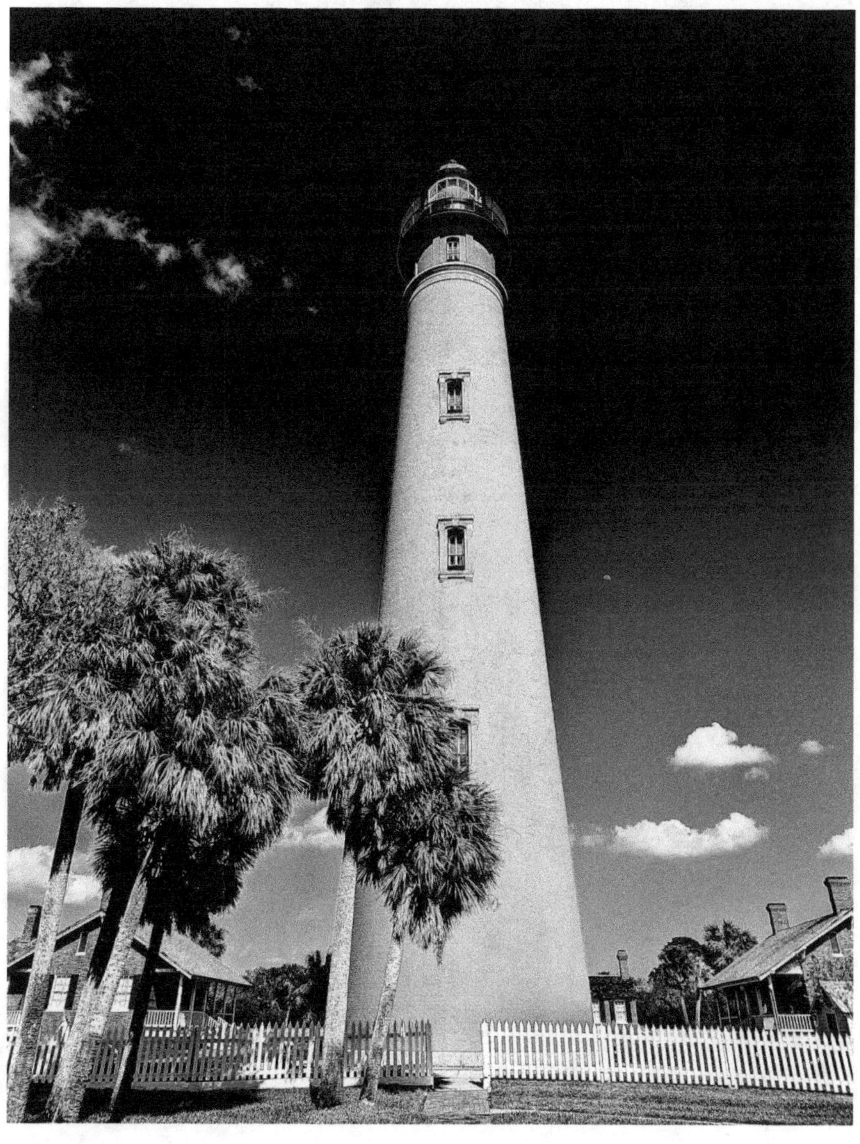

Florida Snow

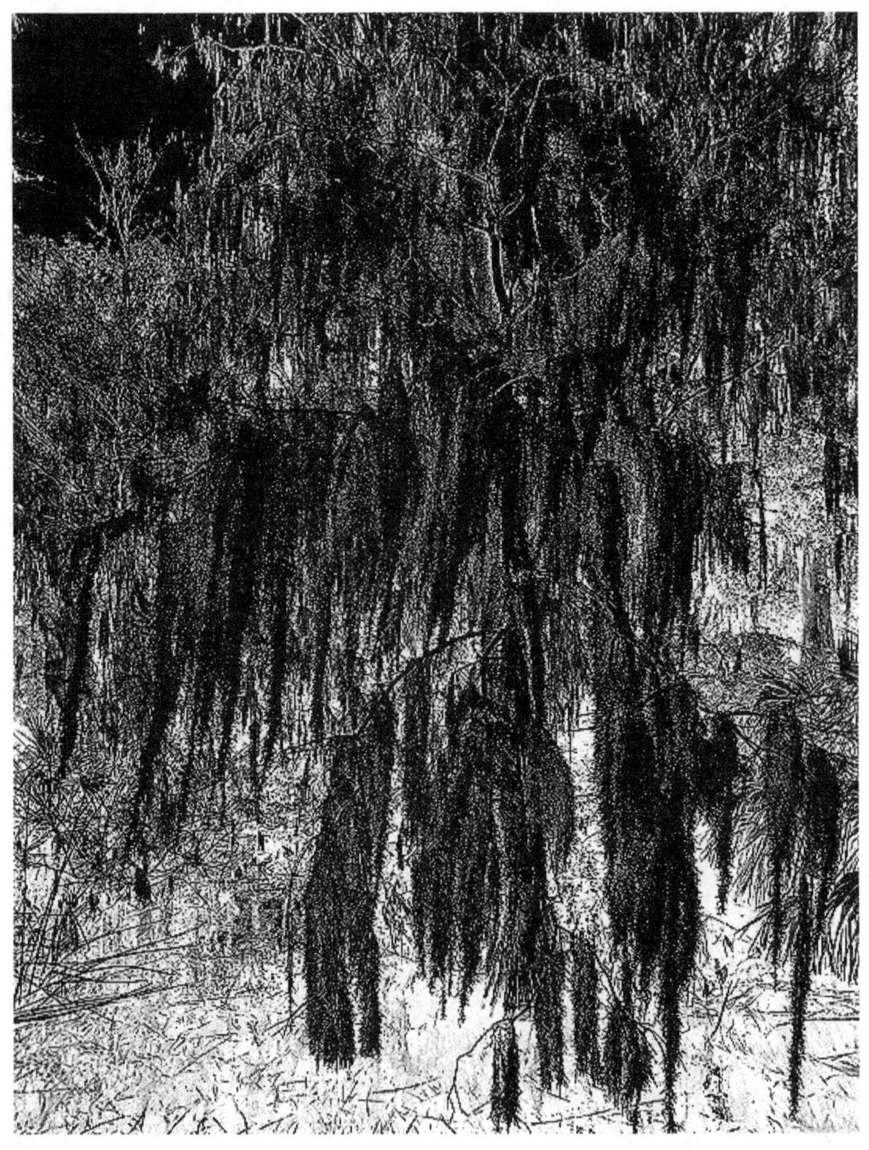

St Augustine Historic District

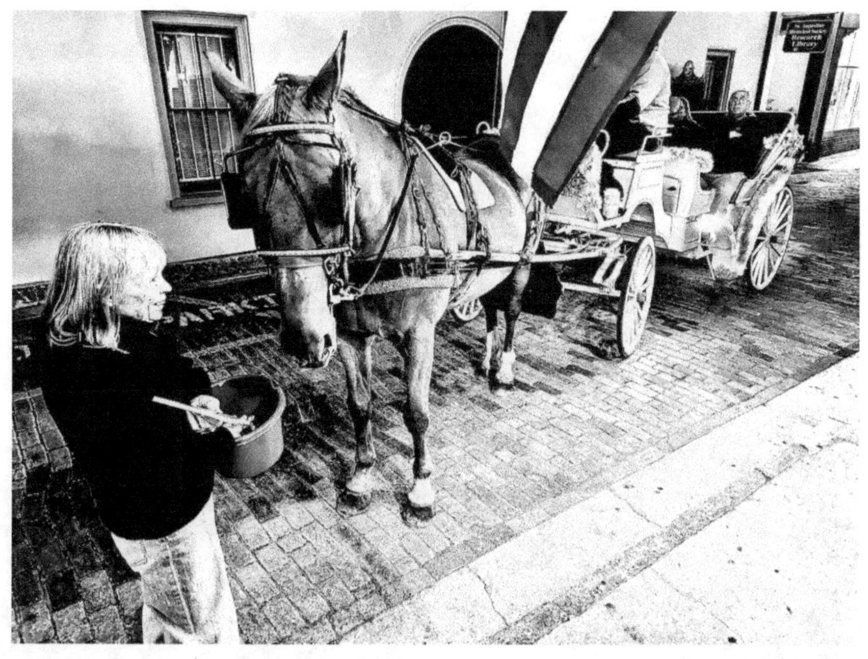

Gemini Springs I

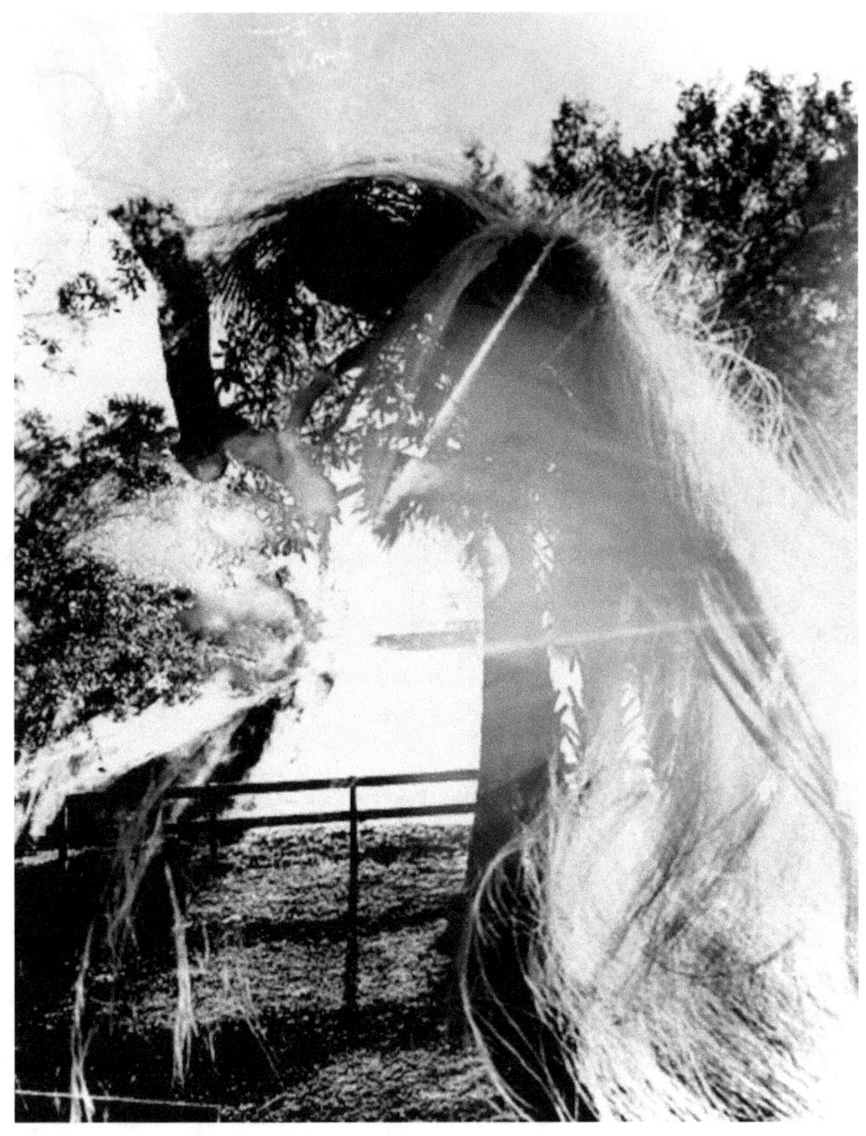

Gemini Springs II

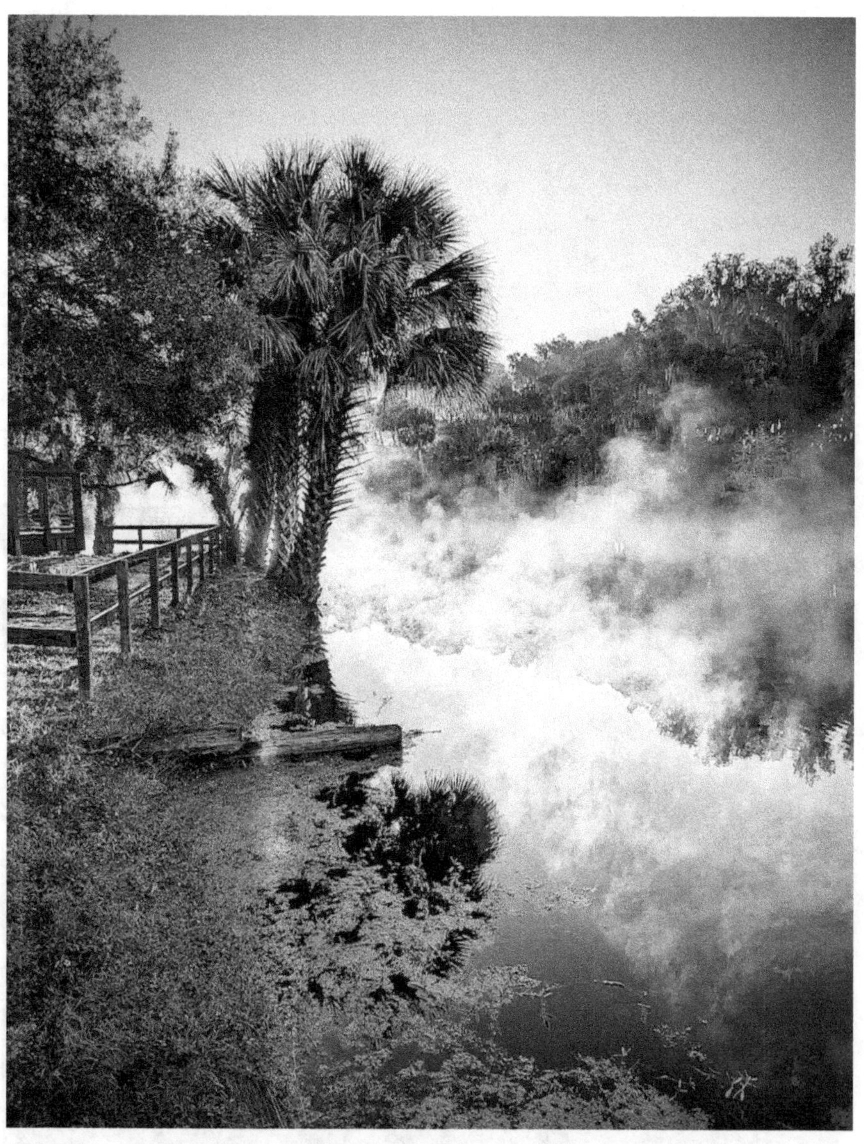

Eliana Vanessa

Schemata

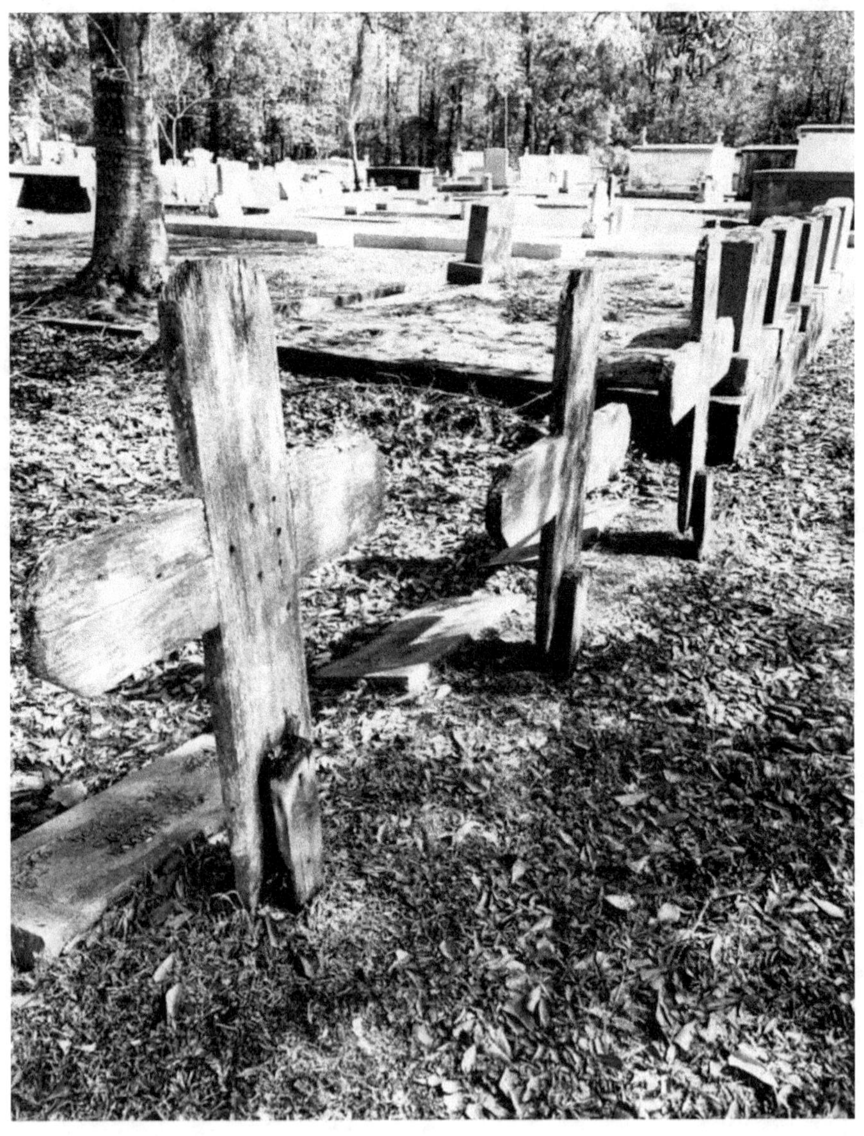

After You

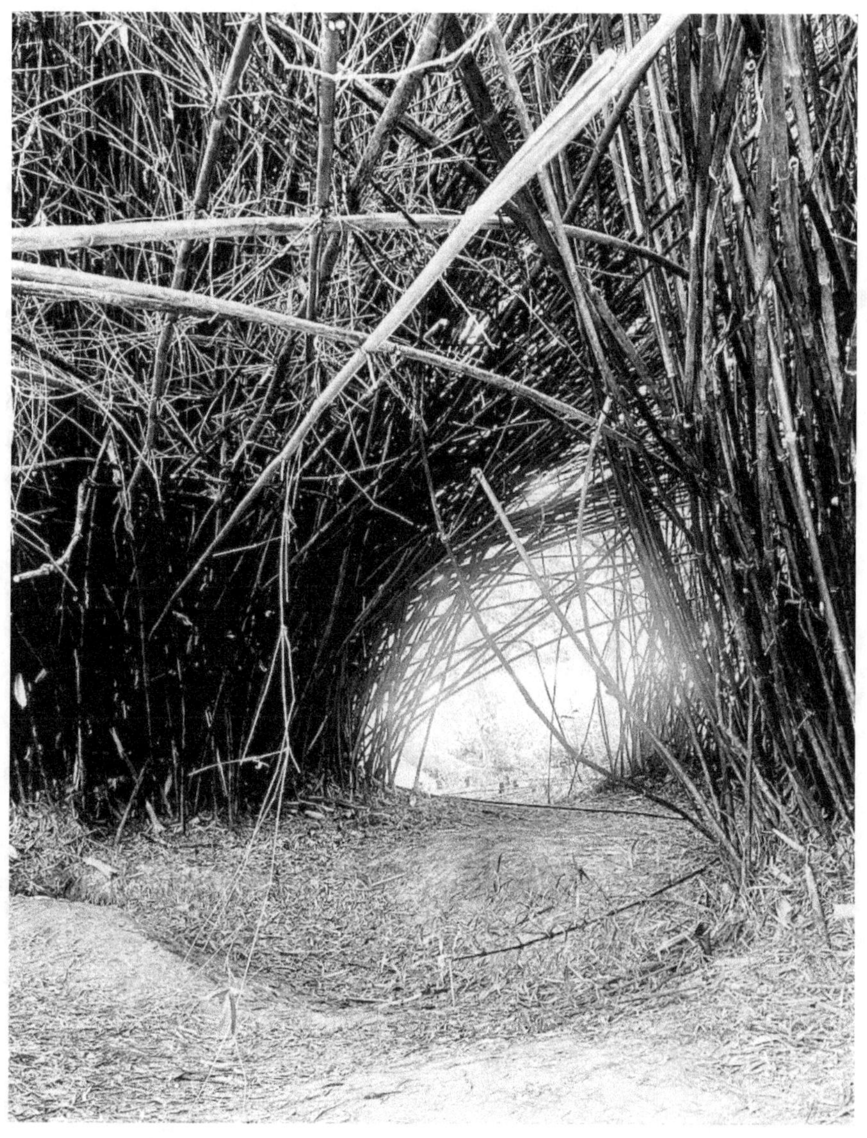

Dearest

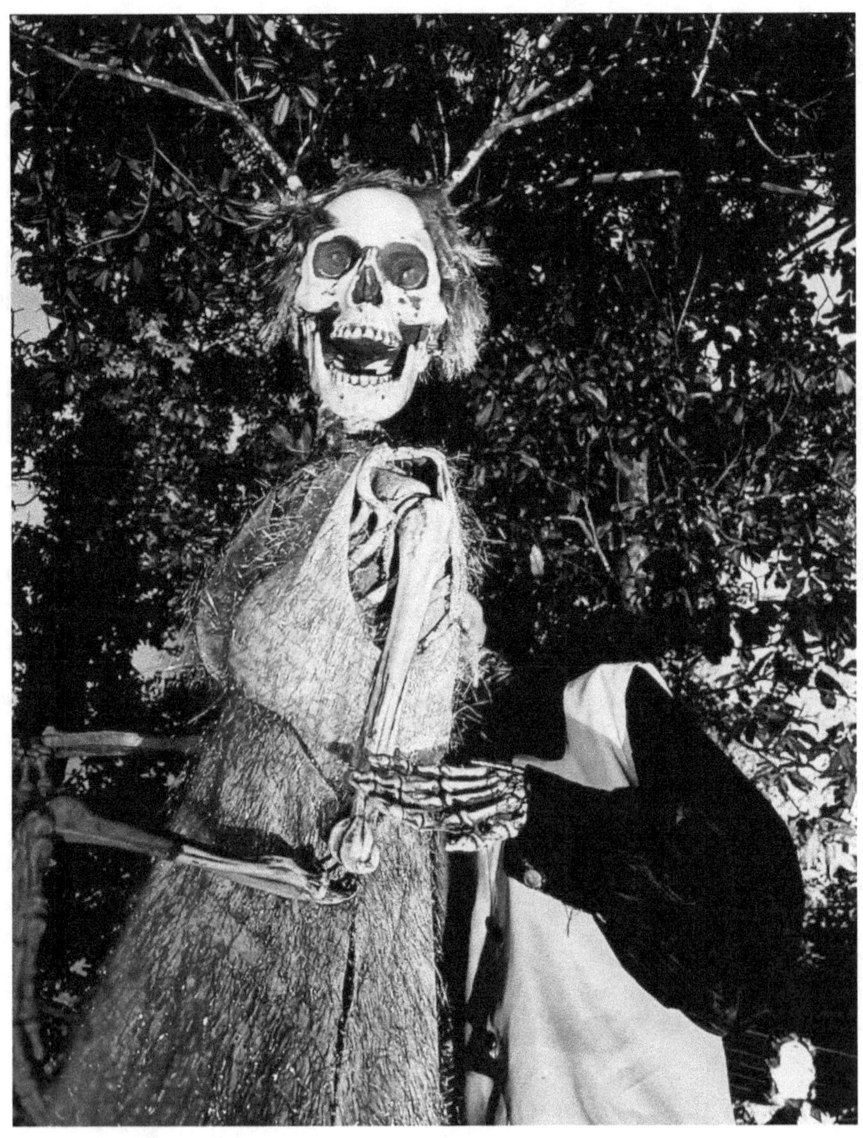

Spiny Branches in Love with Ethereal Night

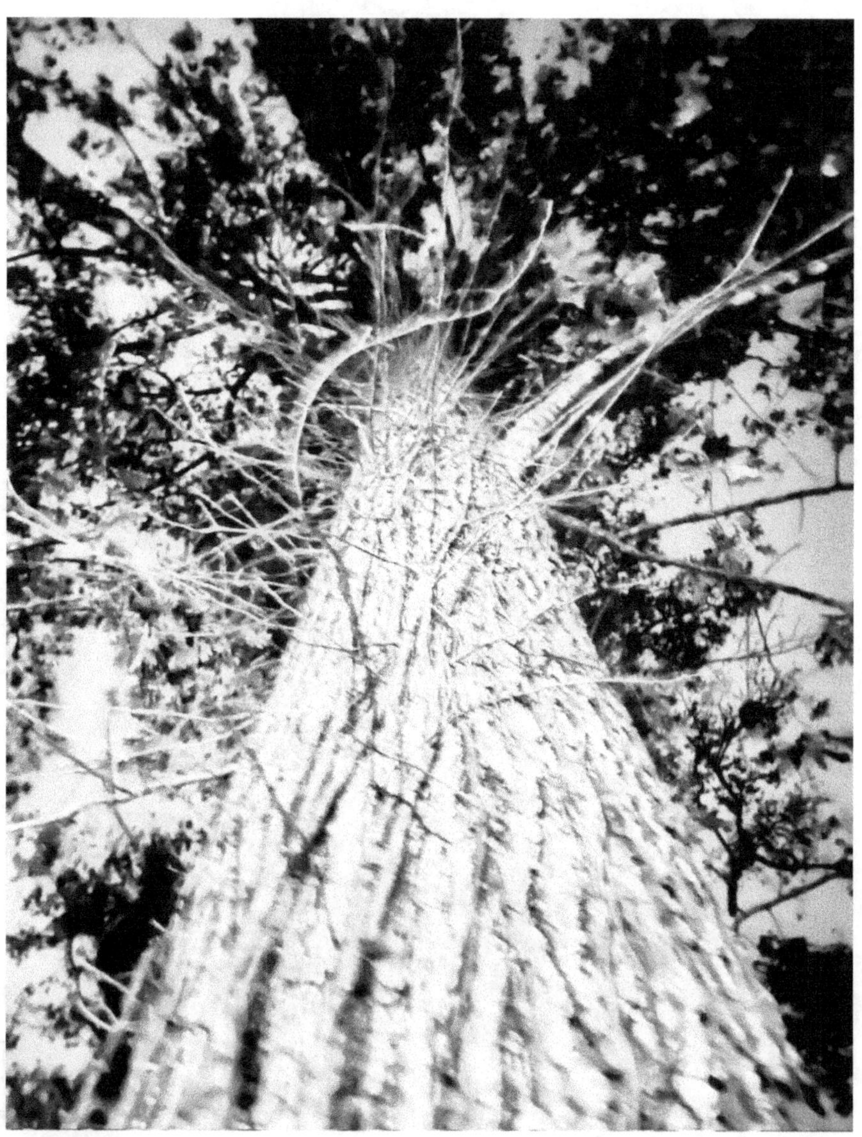

Light Moment

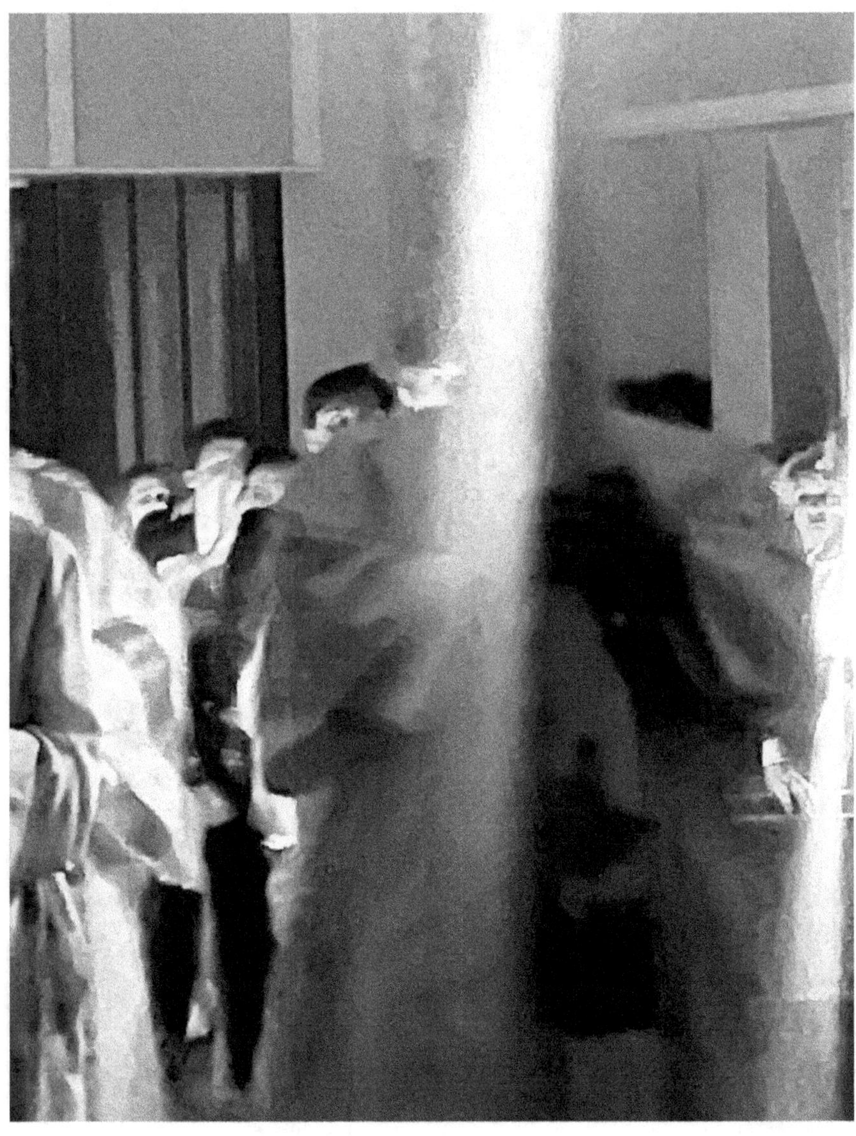

Jeffrey Alfier

Pierre Part, LA

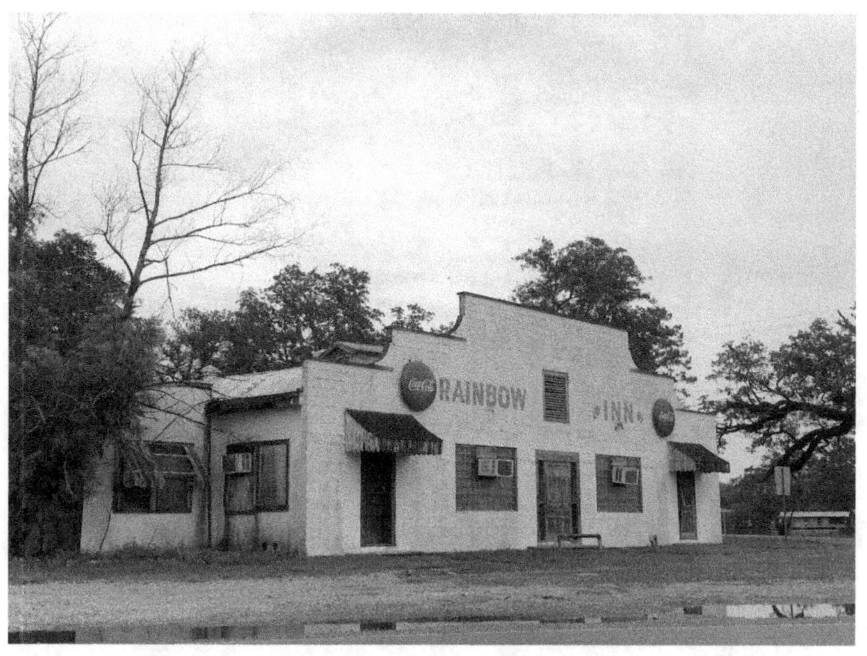

Donaldsonville, LA

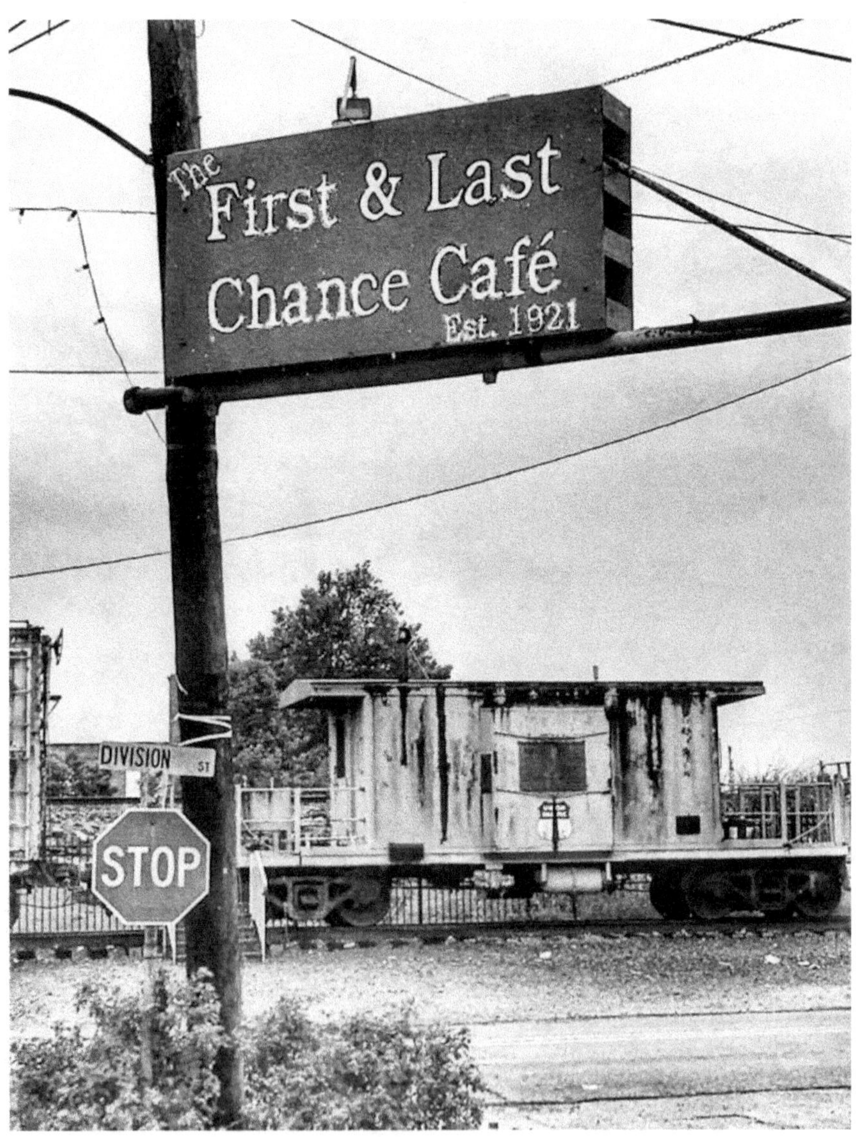

New Iberia 3, LA

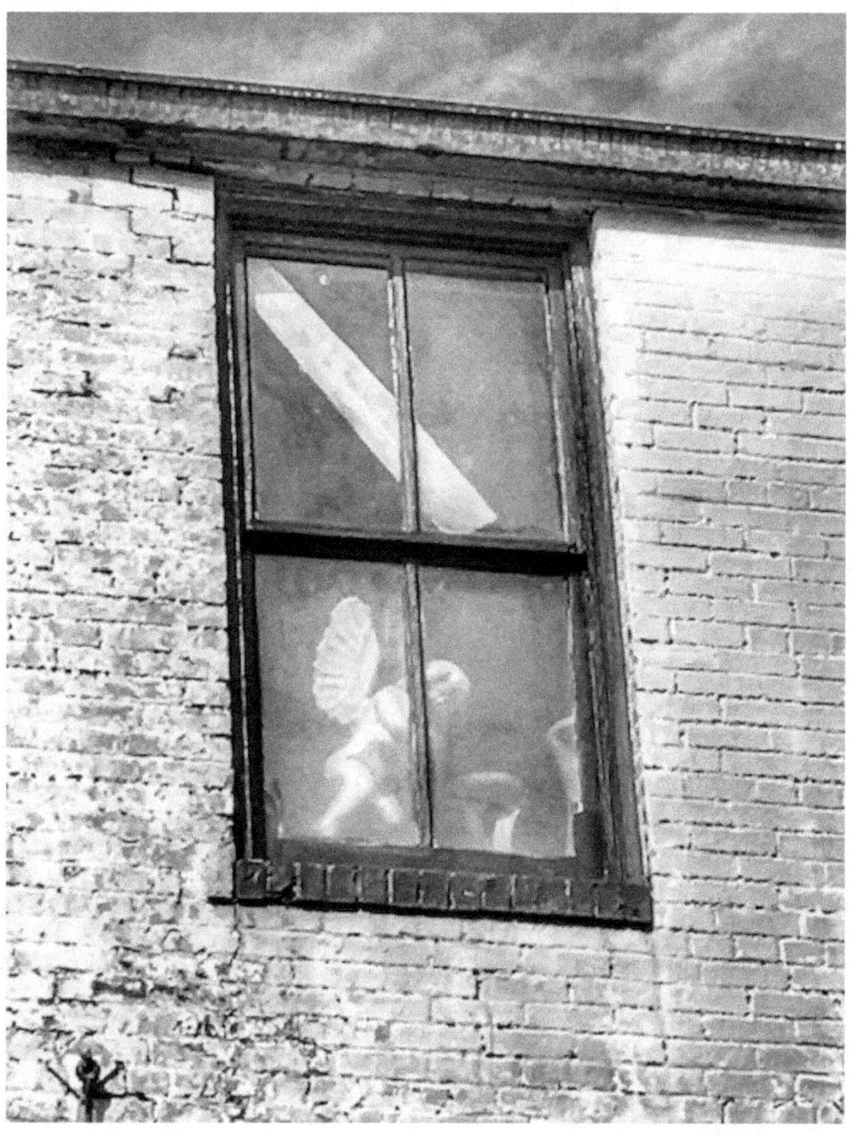

Near French Settlement, LA

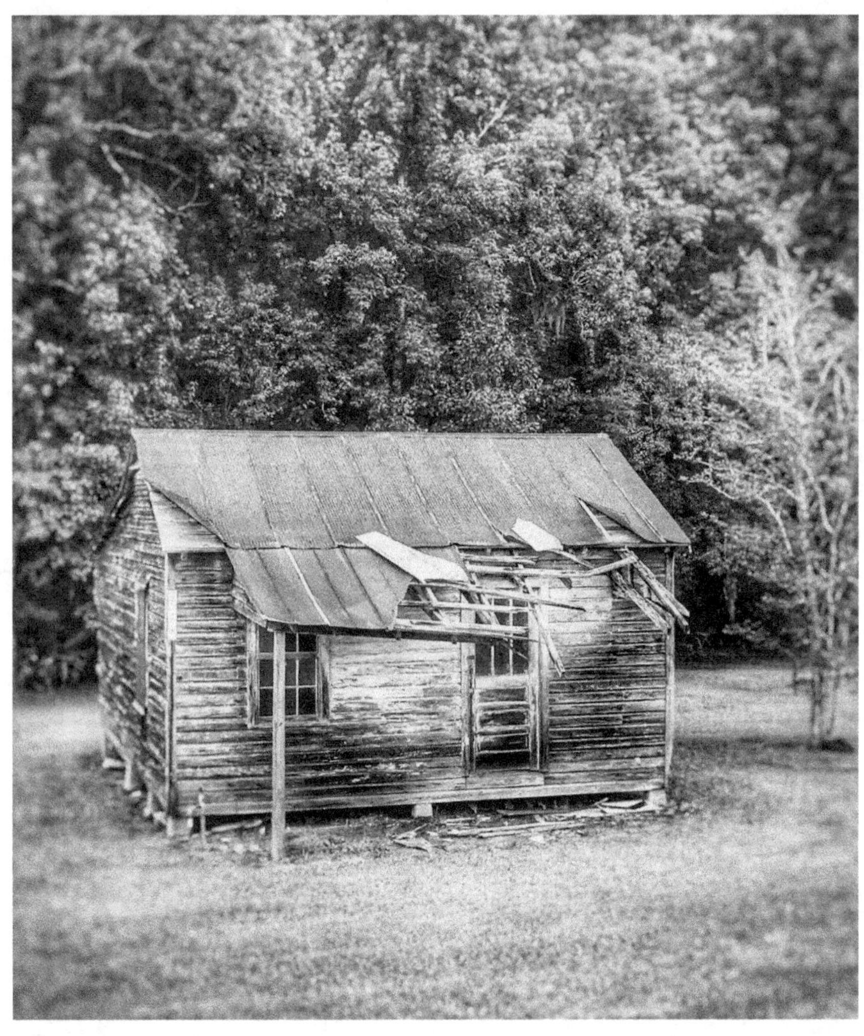

Former Paper Mill New Iberia, LA

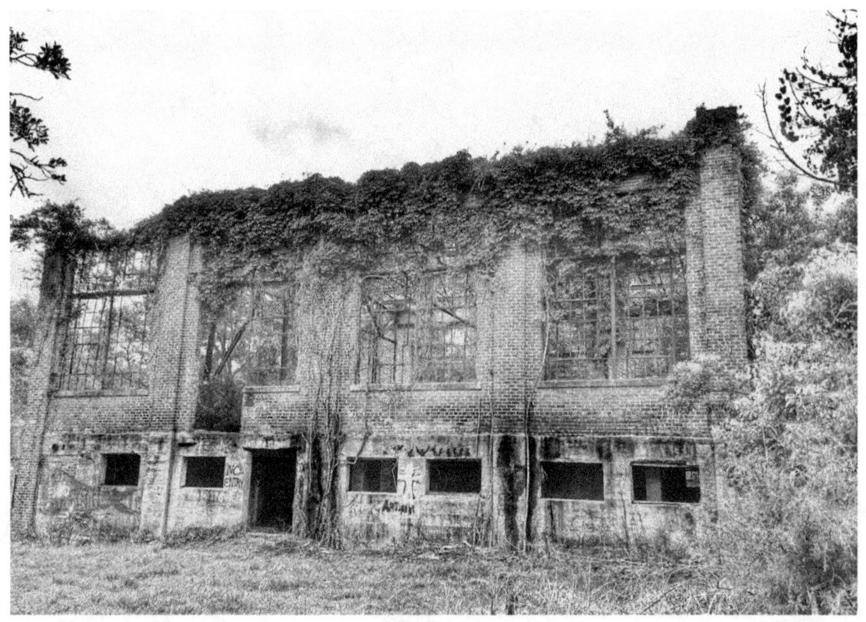

Gerardo Aristimuno

scriptures

after frederick douglas

you pray.
morning, noon and night you pray.
you treasure copies of the scripture.
you walk your place and there they are
at your fingers' tip.
at your kitchen, your sitting room, your night table, your desk, by the rocking table at your porch, and in your toilet rooms.
their pages underlined,
their thinned leaves
translucent at the edges from fingering,
some even stained from coffee —or other drops— and then there is the leather-pocket one
you carry and pull to mitigate your quests,
or soothe your sweats
this time no need to pull it
out your pocket,
just draw your words from memory and say them,
"he that knowseth his master's will and doeth it not,
shall be beaten with many stripes"
then walk towards the pole where
she is tied up, her back and shoulders naked, repeat the words loudly so she hears —louder so you don't hear her pleads—
and punish her till her black skin drips flames
of red from cow-hide lashing;
a uniform new coat of scar over scars.

montgomery, 9/2

memorial

their names
hung from the sky

their voices
not silenced

they rust
In memories of tears

their iron flesh
bleeds into our eyes

we walk under
their shadows

grabbing the choir
of their claim

their banners
as crucifixions

from trees and
bridges tell while burning.

montgomery, 9/2021

travelin light

after alison saar's 1999, bronze installation

alison saar, 1999

(the word is light that travels)

who fears the echoes of these traveling chants
that ring as impatient bells
and resound their defenseless invocations
suspended from oaks of time

soles naked to the sky
doves reaching these feet to sort out their daysprings
to await for the ivies of summer
under the sun's promissory watch

you rock in your ebony suit majestic/ dignified
held by voices/ echoes that own you
and from you spring up
from your mineral chest to be heard
resounding in days spent

you that pass by bring your silence to the stream
to the footprints that mark sorrows and sadness
to the resonance rising from these winged branches
to the shelter of hope halted in time

its enough for you to see
the wounds suffered the march of blood
filling like as a persevering offering
the prodigal cup of hope

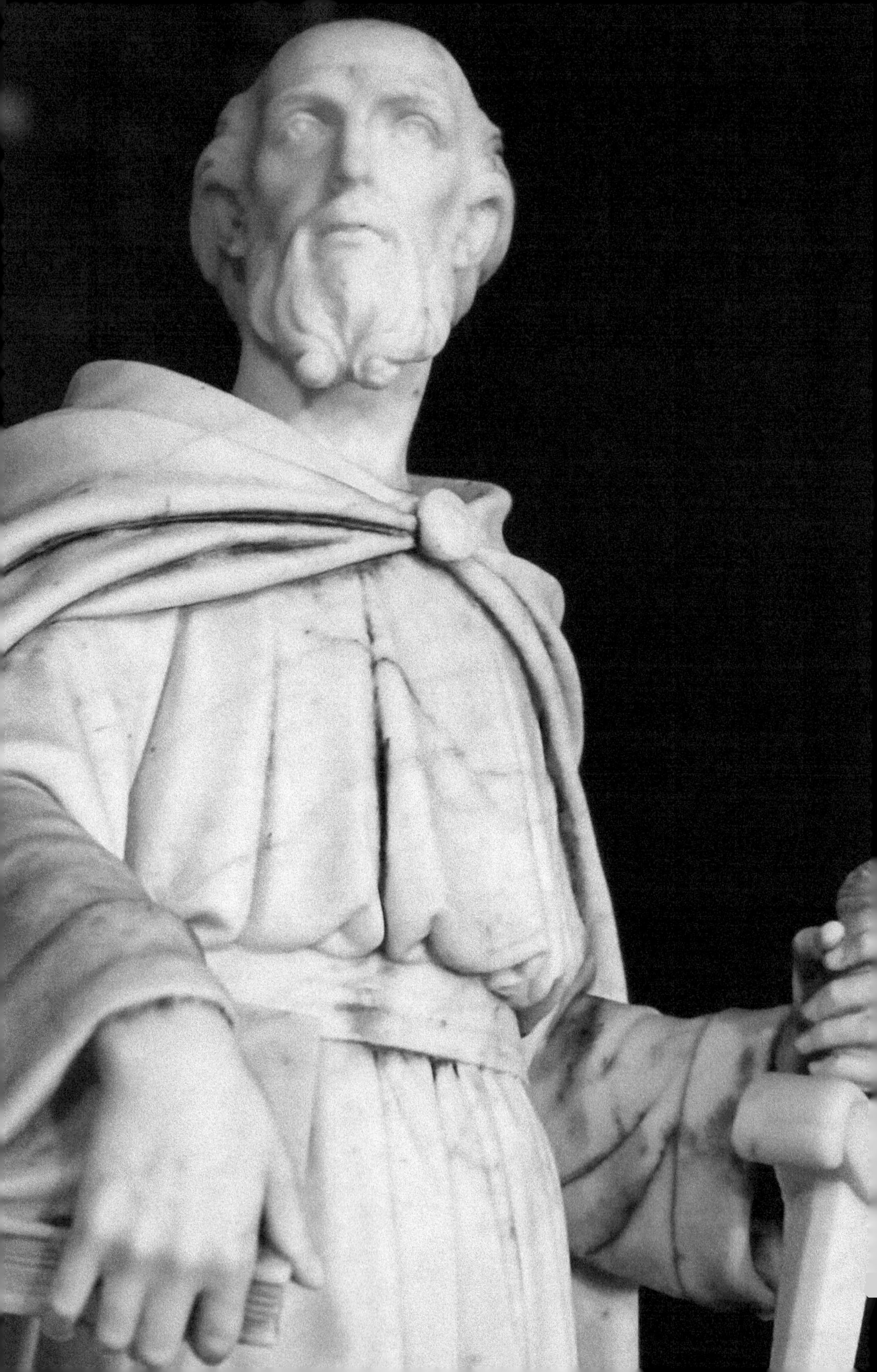

epiphany

that night
january 27, 1956
you found the shoes
in which to walk
the answers you will
wear the next day
and every day till...

the light, the words, the voice.

you found divinity from fear

your agape
from the continuum
of suffering
the road to light
and light itself;
the brotherhood of hope
to carry from auction square
to freedom
from skin to soul
from pray and invocation
to love infinity

mlk,
that night
you felt his touch, his hand,
and let him
take you
as far as truth would carry.

Holly Woodie

behind the levee

innately
up and about,
every dawn
while school
was out for those three measly months,
summer came
through, made
of weeds,
little scorchers,
worn as sun joy
and play
shining well,
with no judgment.

we headed off
with our bicycles
to the sidewinding trails and the glorious paths,
splashing mud, riding as fast as we could up and down muddy trails
through
ankle brush
and over small hills,
like ramps ,
launching us
into the daylit skies
surrounded by ancient trees
and rippling water holes etched into the earth by the overflowing
mississippi.

burning sun
baked us until we were the color
of bark,
swinging into the fast running water, breaking surface

of opaqueness
with no regret,
swimming downstream,
we came through without a scratch!

our wonderland alice knew nothing about swimming
or my hiding spot
in plain sight .

i wriggled away
to be as quiet as a readying pounce,
letting the butterflies pass over,
in a stream of strutting stringed lights,
as the last of the flock headed home.

as often as breath poured open over the playground,
falling
in the wriggling ways of the snakes and gators,
too obtuse
to look back,
my eyes glued shut!

wind and echoes
shifted,
making me forever late for supper,
my one blue dress
drenched
in the wash.

bury me
behind the levee
of New Orleans,
with my pets,
and a life
of palest first bright.

Afreda Hygh

Part I: Knock Knock

Knock, knock
Too
Avoid the rabbit hole
That will send
You somewhere,
Anywhere
On a quest,
a search
for the right
answer
or the right one
to find the truth
to discover your youth
or
you as a
marvel
your own Mona Lisa
an amazing
human artistic genre
wonder
miraculous
Unknown

A Response to *We Wear the Mask* by Paul Laurence Dunbar

Hides
I seek
A way out
or is it away from
That
Which
I
Don't recognize
And doesn't recognized me

As a statue of liberty

Shrouded in dignity
No one knows

The mask even exist
It blends
It becomes one
With what eye imagine
or don't

Hidden humiliation
Should that be my illumination?

Doesn't it look great on
It's better than they want to see

It keeps denial denied

And it foretells nothing or
Does it?

One day
Depending on the day
Becoming the real---deal?

The mask...

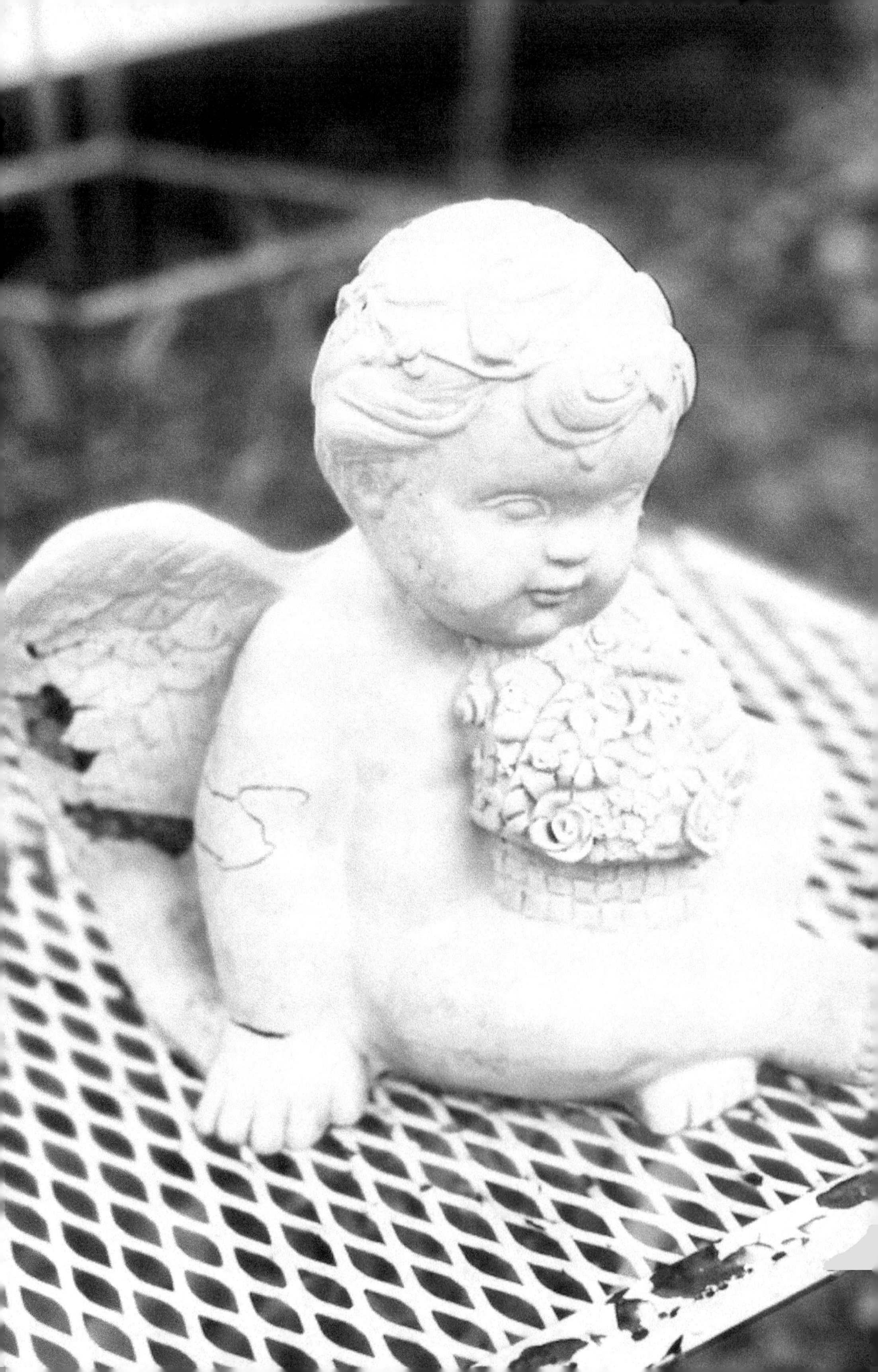

Amalgamation

I don't have to
prove myself to
you
or....*my* power to
you!

My life
is not A Pythagorean
Theorem
The only Thing
I Have To do
Is to Impregnate Myself
With My *Own* ingenious Power
And the light from the heavens above

And the right
To be
free
Within my ancient
soul
to soar
uninterrupted
Eternally

Chad Foret

The Infrared Universe Unfolds

I like when you sing like an ant
driven mad by its love for okra.

All you've ever wanted was to wake up
with shoulders wide as Mary Shelley's.

Some red-eared sliders sun on stones
& the wooden foundations of washed

away homes & diced cork island art. When
the rain starts, let's stay, mistake the small

black rocks for baby crickets while mist
whips move in waves. Later, in the dark,

I'll slowly reconstruct a rotted CPAP
headset strap, pray you stay asleep.

The plaza statue's purple oyster eyes
are still intact, the path to all pearl.

Poem with a Line by Audrey

1

After Ida, the Boutte/Houma exit eagle

nests disappeared, the only monument
outside of swampland for several miles.

Groups of smashed, small treetops east

of I-51 seem superheated from the pale,
broken points. The western Hahnville

high school gym wall collapsed. We help

Craig move vinyl & boards from his yard
& somehow no one steps on the nails

in the neighbor's upside-down ceiling

complete with fan. Craig gives frozen
frozen garfish patties, happy to have

us here. We will decorate his boat for

a future Blessing of the Fleet, maybe
in Des Allemandes, long before we all

die of an addiction to feeling useful.

2

Japanese maple leaves hide their waxy

backs which seem redder when the wind

blows. Every morning, I kiss some chemical
sugars, draining Grayhawk, adoring the deep

greens of Mona lavender. Your Spanish
architecture fetish was always floating

there just waiting to be told, & curd is indeed
everything you want butter to be. When you

smuggle loose jam from the English Tea
Room off Rutland in your purse, I feel

like we've just left the last movie train
& do not look back, but the train does.

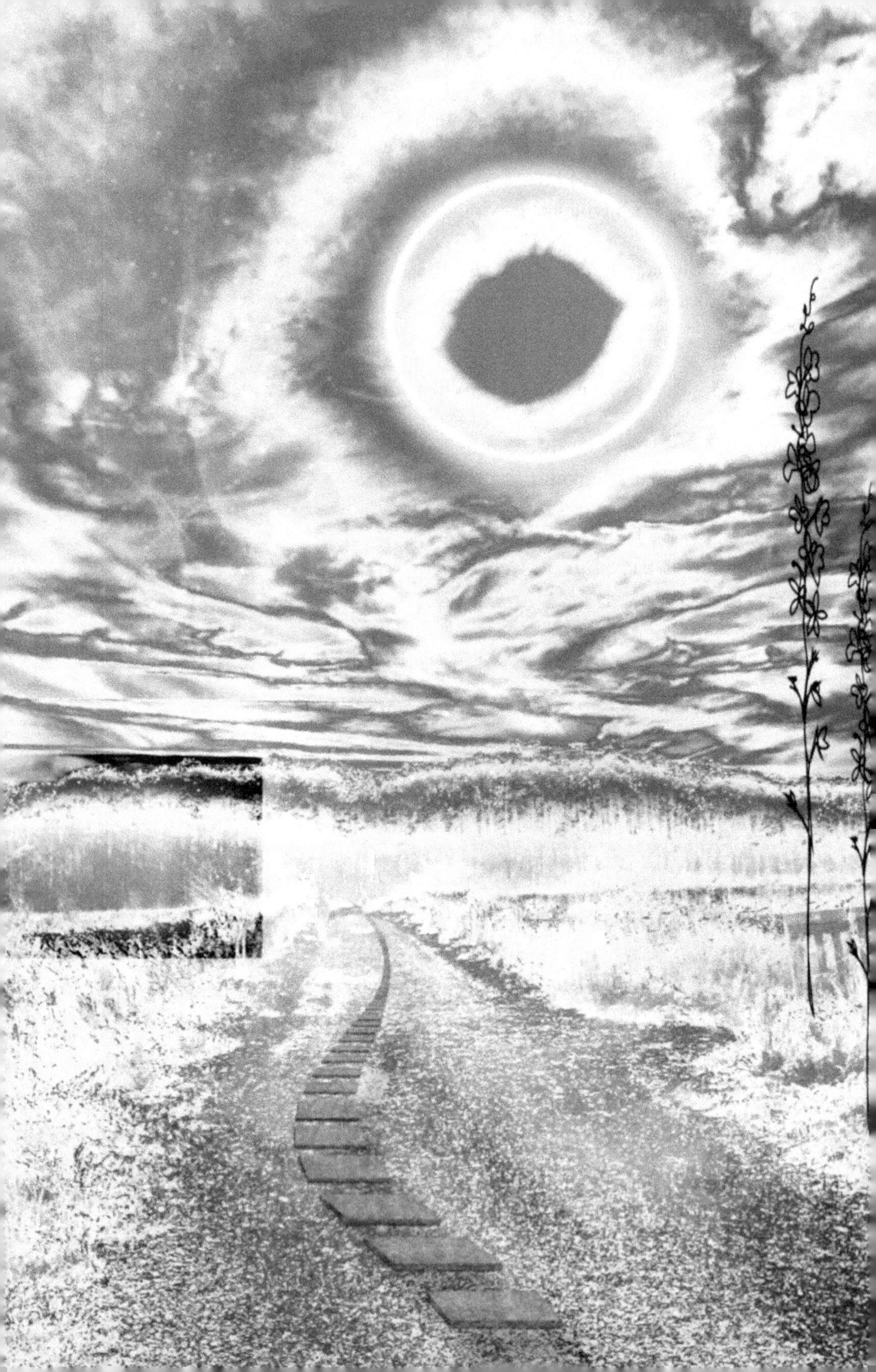

Virtually Reality

after Mary Ruefle

Blue tick, bless the basil, paw sweet mint soil, hose reels
heaven to a crane fly. Pine needles sway like sea plants,
stuck in netting, coop enclosures. The owl's eyes are ear-

wax, the color of raincoats in a room with no windows.
Ants make foam in a Maine Coon's mouse halves. Squirrels
break acorns on a swollen fence post until orange spills

everywhere, like an 80s kitchen with transparent purses,
short cord rice cookers, the orange vase full of moldy sun-
flowers, pity for the honey pots stuck between orange

& beige. In the country, there's always someone waiting
to be unhappy on a beach, to owl like a comma in the oak,
suspension the tongue can depend on. Who knows what

you need? First it was algae blooms smokers

& speckled trout should fear, now all touch.
When they pry you from the petrified couch,

a pearl appears. Not farming is the happiest

thing in the world. The field is like the ground
where a temple was, & when there's a cloud-

burst you can be anywhere. You're never alone

with the earth & your curiosity. You have time
for friends & they love that about you. I always

loved a hunter who enters the air, grips the whisper

of a rat, the burned field unfolding at someone's will.
There are fourteen acres of floodlight within each coyote.
How can you breathe here where everyone awakens dazed

in a pig mask? I couldn't name another seabird, not even
the pelican choking on my childhood. Sad dogs survive
long enough to be the only option. In the country, snow-
flakes fall so fast I can plant a Kieffer pear by chance.

Alton Paul Baker, Jr.

Bayou Sauvage

On a humid Louisiana evening
I paddle along
the sun dappled waterway
under the old moss-laiden oaks.

A king fishes for a living
Like a dive bomber on the mark
Finding his fish.

The ancient one
Basks in the sun
As he yawns framing the bandit who washes his crawfish
While a red-tailed death glider watches.

The is but a snapshot
of the heaven
I yearn to find
on my evening
on Bayou Sauvage.

Belle River Scavengers

As ancient Guardians of the swamp
Patrol the waters and the wise bard Predator
surveys his domain from his lofty perch.

I quietly paddle my pirogue through
the dimly lit foggy morning mazes of the swamp.

I go from tree to tree looking for the best
places to put my traps and set them with care
for the harvest of the Belle River scavengers.

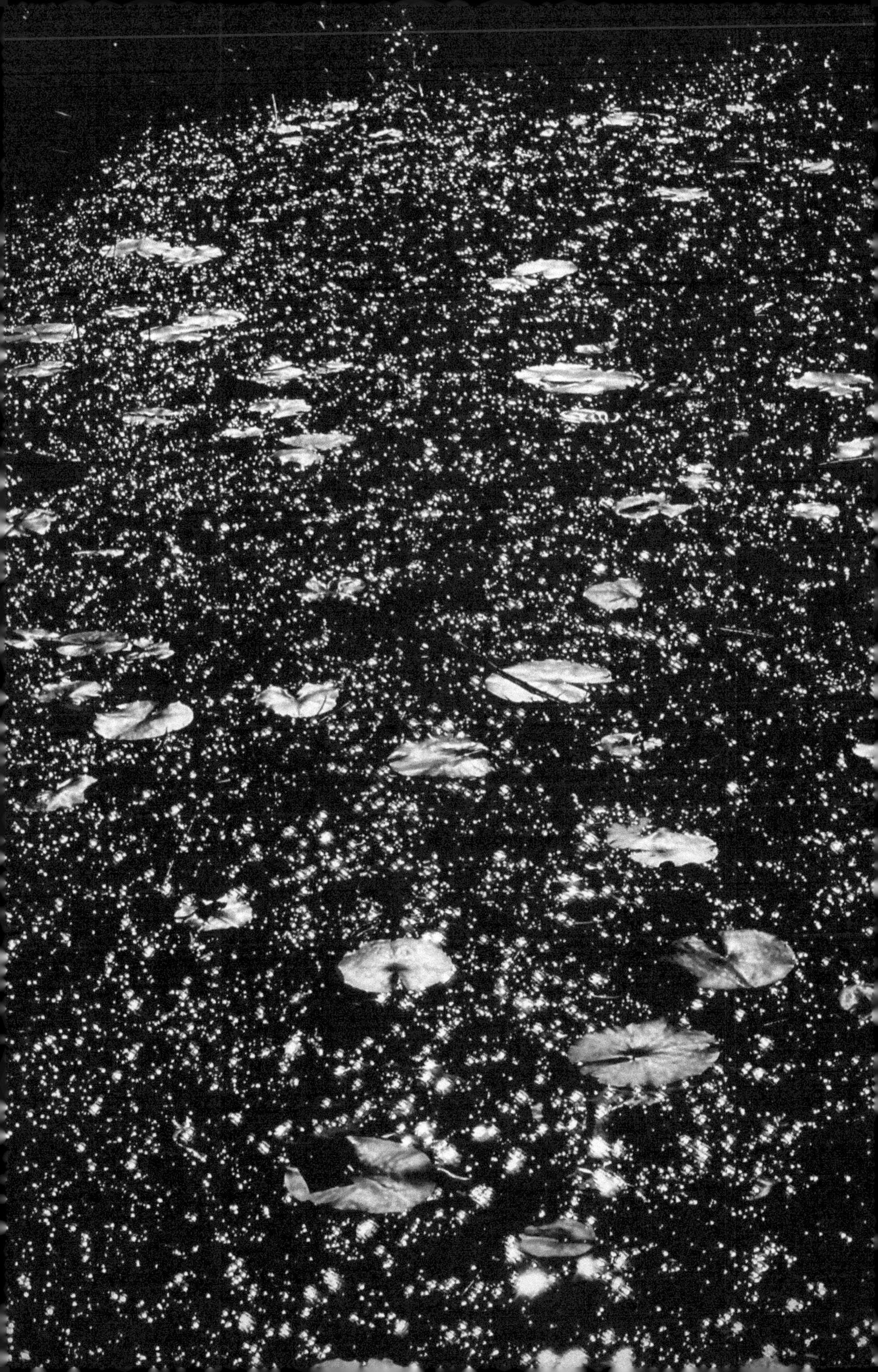

Dionne Charlet Baker

Preserve

He tickles with wishes
from a swirl a silt
glopped up by a melee
of sunfish above Pontchartrain.

Insert the however
above Lepomis cyanellus
consuming fungal tidbits
nestled over gypsum
like ash wafting from St. Helens
devoured by the ninth ward
of his "trash fish"
stunted as perch overpopulate our pond
once seeded with bass
he caught while guarding Beau Chene.

There is only never in his eyes
tranquil with the waterline
and dome of sky
beaded in refraction
and dilated round each pupil.

Fisherman for sport
would drain this pond
three years departed
to seed it with catfish
or some other trophy
to the now that casts,

but here overgrown with branches and words
the invasive thrive
medallioned in silver

irised in blue
just past the head
as green glimmers to gray.

Priory of Lutea

She mantles
the rosary of her lore
across the flooded forest
of Barataria
with a brush dipped
and dripping Nelumbo.

Biding the pigments,
she centers the priory
of her canvas
beneath fronds of marsh
where the brackish yields
to kneeling cypress
stumped in congregation
before the rebirth of the lotus.

Moon-blown nymphal fingers,
each a welded swan in mourning,
filigree strokes of swamp
from rhizome and silt,
filtering the apex
gar and moccasin
to crown the dome of stomata
within the eddies of the mist.

Ringlet afloat, fragrant, perfection,
her tepals echo tongues of the East
where tolerance of choice
rises from the murk
to hatch from a clutch,
find solace in hisses,
and seek every soul in bloom.

PHILLIP T. KEHOE

Ti-enny

It was about the fifth or sixth time she had called her young daughter from the front stoop of the pale blue shotgun cottage on Mazant Street. But this time she used her big voice, the one a cousin swore she could hear from across the river in Algiers.

Her mama's "big voice" penetrated the deep sleep Ti-enney had been enjoying in the small laundry yard at the back of the house that was hung with four lines of wash from fence to fence in the too still air that sang of a storm coming. Little Ti-enney had been eating the sweet-tart kumquats from the neighbor's tree when she first got tired and curled up in the fence corner and began to dream again about the pink threads of cotton candy her daddy had bought for her out at Lincoln Beach. She sat bolt upright out of that sweet dream when she heard that voice of her mama's but that did not mean she was fully awake yet.

She yawned deeply to rouse herself and that breath was filled with the flavor of her mama's red beans cooking and that pulled her right out of her slumber and put her right as to the place and day it was. It was then that Ti-enney jumped up and ran towards the kitchen door. She knew that if her mama used that big voice twice, it might just be followed by the whistle of a willow switch aimed at the back of her knees.

Slapping through her daddy's still damp work pants as she ran, something stopped her stock still. A chill as real as January grabbed her by the spine. She looked down at the gray-brown packed river silt of the yard and not four feet in front of her was a patch that looked more like the red clay of the north shore under the dappled shade of a mimosa tree. The copperhead lifted its eyes towards hers. That is when Ti-enney realized that she had a voice every bit as big and as powerful as her mama's.

The Only Ways

Pace and place
Was plain to see Linguistically
Stylistically
Mystically
Rattling akimbo through No. 2
On soul skewed
Stone walks
River bound
or lake bound
Up or down
Are the only ways
To Navigate
The twisted history
That lies between Bucktown and Algiers Bywater and
The River Shack Unless, of course,
You converse
With Marie.

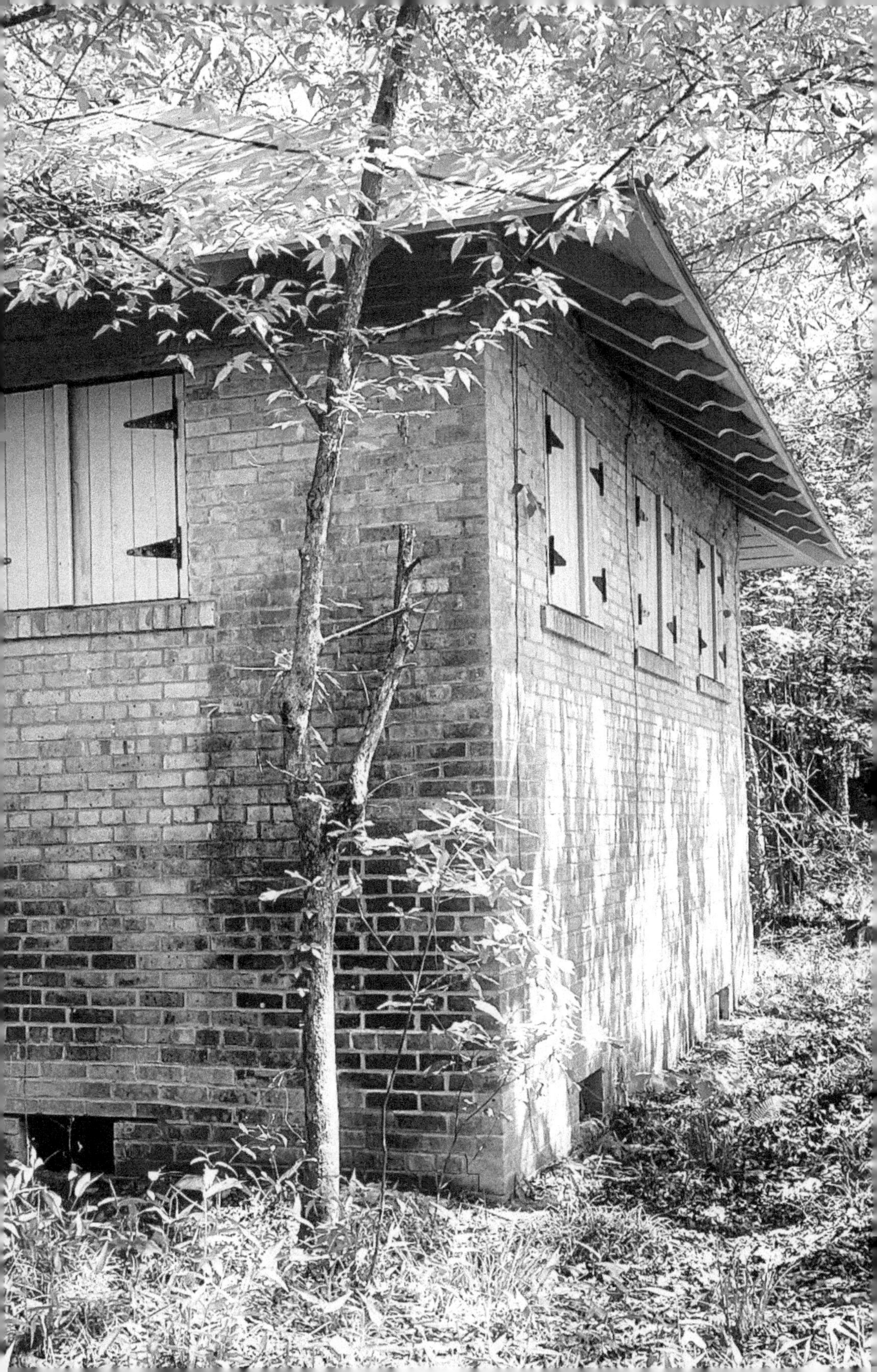

To be read on Fat Tuesday

Tomorrow the crystal goblets
and go cups will have gone dry.
The Crescent City no longer
reverberating with sirens call of
throw me something mister.

The music of Aaron's arias will be gone,
along with Indian chants, mid-city marching bands
and downtown disco ditties for the high steppers.
Music offered up in transportable tongues
of rose garnet opacity that whisk dreams afroth
into a brand new deja vous.

From Tipitina's to the Rivershack
to the R-Bar, St. Roch's and B.J.'s
a sigh will rise with the remains of today

Beads will yet hang with Spanish Moss on
Live Oak limbs swinging so low and with
discarded garments on balcony railings.

King Cakes and Hurricanes will be traded for
cafe au lait and beignets and seven Fridays of
Catholic catfish with all the trimmings.

Feathers and sequins will decorate the town
from the river up the neutral grounds,
yet no coconut left behind will be found.

Midnight will bring the last parade
of mounted police through The Quarter
sweeping streets free of carousers from Cleveland
or Conway or Clovis, shooing them back to
Fat City and Airline Highway motels.

After Rex retreated to The Sheraton and
Comus to The Marriot and after the din has passed,
the locals will have flocked to their own courtyards
and parlors to await a dawn as quiet as cooling ash.

Sweet Olive's scent will replace
that of humanities excess.
Jasmine will return as the true gold
of the old neighborhoods.

Some big chief in Treme will awaken
thinking to himself: maybe tomorrow is
soon enough to start a new suit. Maybe purple.

Yet, my orange zest memory
of his suit from this year has
added yet another layer to my
doberge life as reminder.
Never, ever should one
Cease To Love

Russell MacClaren

Mississippi River Pilot

Man of the river,
say not to the water:
"I have sampled your wetness
and tasted the delights that bubble from your reeds and rushes.
I know
the danger and power
that roils in your depths,
therefore I have made you."
Man of the river,
open up your heart.
See the truth!
You have not made the river. The river has made you.

Water Has Memory

Moon tides conjure waves that wash driftwood, shells and Spanish moss,
up on the muddy banks.
The moon regales in
women of fond desires, werewolves howling by the river, lovers kissing
beneath foam spray.
Breakers crash upon the shore, across the moon's imaginings. Froth
filters through the cypress, and the water remembers.

Lazy Pontchartrain Afternoon

Nature holds me easy in her heart
as beards of clouds turn white and then depart. Propeller planes drone
on this lazy afternoon, beneath the sun, beside the pale moon...
Gaggles of kiddos stretch out on the land, beneath umbrellas that
sprinkle pale sand. They hug near castles to drink their lemonade beside
the teens who bask within the shade.
I wax nostalgic remembering a day
of circling horses with a giant Zephyr at its play, when life was a journey
we all muddled through
with wishes and daydreams and nothing much to do.

Pontchartrain Evenings

Fishermen huddle near oil lamps
that dot the curving sea wall.
Water slaps the concrete steps
as harvesters cast nets into the brine, dragging shrimp, fish, octopus and crabs to metal tubs made cool with bags of ice.
Passersby spin tales of tarpons,
sharks and whales, then gather leavings from those who fish along the walk.
Newfound friends leave for home with stories and thoughts a jumble,
food to fill their stomachs,

words to flavor gumbo.

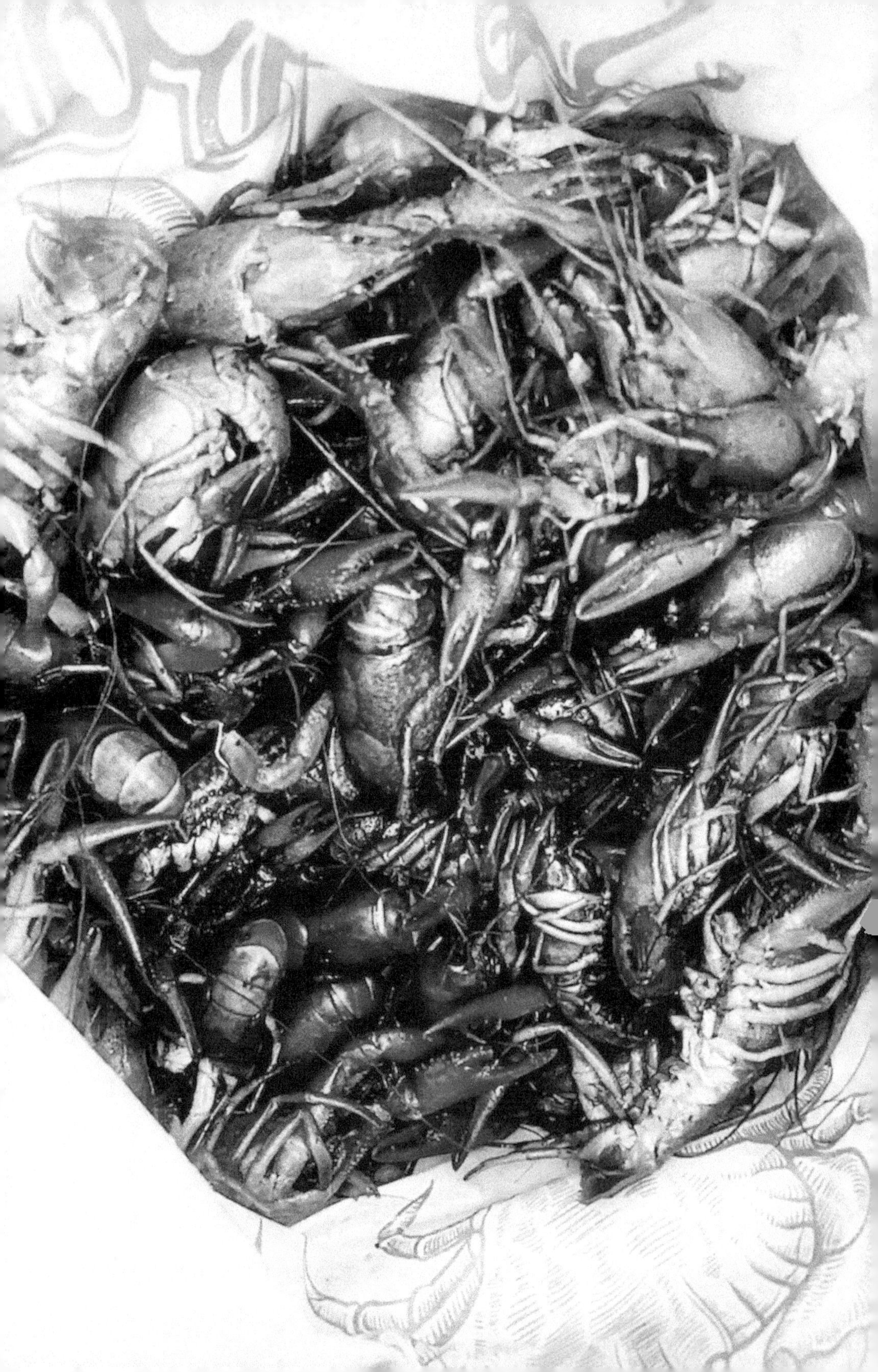

Gina Ferrara

Light Montage

We caught the streetcar to see Downtown decorated,
neon and bright wattage of the Saenger,
individual and collective bulbs
advertising shows in stellar signage,
emitted electric plumage of a proud peacock.
The fluorescent marquis listed
a Donna Summer tribute at the Joy
followed by Dumpsta Phunk
and trunks of palm trees swathed
in pluralized white light.
You grabbed my hand
when we saw the man, the deft work
of his fists punching the night
in jabs, uppercuts, quick little defenses
against imaginary enemies
beneath the bridge blocking the real glimmer
always given by stars.

As of a River

On the levee's perilous side,
a solitary, dwindling batture,
the heron stands with unspoken triumphs
and transgressions,
an indigenous glyph, unbending,
mythical, white,
near the great river's mouth,
agape, filling and emptying itself,
the muddied swirl, the inscrutable alluvial
the mystery of silt, sweeps quick centuries
swallows the epochs

too swift, too muddy to hold our reflections.

Sequence 12/24

Earlier I walked through gravel.
My ruby red lizard heel
sticks as it gleams
in the sidewalk crack,

fear of falling,
fear of the man on the bike
butter yellow
supple leather seat the color of a camel
or mohair fringe.

Dressed in a suit
with his empty basket,
he pedals faster.
In the dark I am running
avenues, a taut seam's length

Light will not unfold like a page
dog-eared, not now.

I only want to get home
to makeshift topiaries,
the iron bench wrought
with virtuosity,

the camellias on both sides of the porch
always burdens on the bush
the inevitable soft petal plunge,
blossoms spent, scattered
touching blades.

The Same Result

Between manic and hollow
on that spectrum,
that's where some laughter registers
in all its rapidity, volume filling rooms,
joy-void
too eager, too quick,

exposed box-cutter
blade too ready to inflict,
taking me on a retro ride
the amusement park, then,
next to the tilt-a-world
topsy-turvy neon tumult, distant calliopes and cacophonies
the haunted house,
a rickety red car,
hesitant, inching along the tracks
desperate
hinges doors
flinging to the dark corridor
where the horror was always ahead.

Liquids from Childhood Remembered

Rarely solidified, mystery
arrived in ounces marked like lacerations,
between lethal and medicinal,

tinctured with the unspoken,
a scant stream of warmth,
unearthed bitter roots dulled the cramps,

the utmost kept in a rusted can,
dissipating skull and bones, obliterated color, volatile,
sparingly applied to chamois or last winter's flannel,

behind the hinged mirror door,
uncapped viscosity swallowed nameless, no residual evergreen scent
yet known, to steady a quivering hand,

inhaled ammonia a shade of tarnished
tears, discretion sized, in the cinched velvet pouch,
reviving a mother, a daughter, sister, or aunt

or the sweet digestif, not meant to quench,
the steady swallow, serene as an emerald and watered mint,
served in the best blue depression glass.

CONTRIBUTORS

Susan S. Newton's first book, "A Single Woman's Survival: Hurricane Katrina" is a gripping memoir of her experience at that tumultuous time. Available at Amazon.com.
"The 7th Rainbow" is Susan's first poetry chap book, and is available directly from her. See below.
She is currently working on a second poetry book, encompassing more of her original poems.
Contact her at: sntechsvcs@gmail.com

Tobi Alfier is published nationally and internationally. Credits include War, Literature and the Arts, The American Journal of Poetry, KGB Bar Lit Mag, Washington Square Review, Cholla Needles, James Dickey Review, Gargoyle, Permafrost, Arkansas Review, Anti-Heroin Chic, and others. She is co-editor of San Pedro River Review (www.bluehorsepress.com).
https://www.facebook.com/tobi.cogswell

William R. Gallaher ("Bill") has been writing since 1976, while on the faculty of the LSU School of Medicine. He first published poetry in 2012, now totaling 16 titles on Amazon over a range of subjects and styles. Born and raised in NYC Metro, with Harvard Ph.D., he is the adopted son of New Orleans, now residing in the Northshore wetlands.
Social media contacts:
https://www.facebook.com/bill.gallaher.14/
Amazon author page:
https://www.amazon.com/stores/author/B01LZDVHW9/

Valentine Pierce, the Writer-in-Residence at a Studio in the Woods in 2006, has been writing most of her life — poetry, prose, essays, journalism and more. Recent publications include the *New Orleans Poetry Journal* and "Rigorous Magazine." *Her book Up Decatur: Second Edition.*
Co-hosting Rhythm & Muse, Berkeley Museum in the early 2000s, set

her on the path to producing poetry programs throughout New Orleans.
Amazon link for *Up Decatur: Second Edition*
My Book
Facebook Link
https://www.facebook.com/valentine.pierce

A Friend of the Egrets
Kendall Elizabeth Smith is a December 2023 graduate of The University of Louisiana at Lafayette with plans to further her education in January 2024 at Southeastern Louisiana, Hammond in their Masters of Business Administration program. Kendall is a classical pianist beginning her love of music at age five; she also enjoys creating original works of art.

Isabella MacDonald Smith is the author of "Ancient Memories," a novel based on historical facts of her family's life in the mid-1600's in Ireland and Spain. She is also the author of "Skip and Axel Rossi" and "On the Other Side."

Dennis Formento lives in Slidell, Louisiana, USA, near his native New Orleans. His books of poetry include *Spirit Vessels* (FootHills Publishing, 2018), *Looking for An Out Place* (FootHills, 2010), and *Cineplex* (Paper Press, 2014.) Edited Mesechabe: *The Journal of Surregionalism, 1991-2001*. He has collaborated locally with musicians including his own Frank Zappatistas free jazz/free verse project, and in Italy with the renowned "avant-folk" group Duo Bottasso. He has organized readings for the world-wide network, 100,000 Poets for Change, in New Orleans and St. Tammany Parish, LA since 2011. In 2023 he won the poetry category of the Wisdom-Faulkner literary competition with his manuscript, *Phaeton's Wheels*.

Cynthia Schaefer is the author of *Present Peace: A Poetry Collection*. She is a former accountant and a CPA, who recently has taken a career shift into education, teaching children with dyslexia to read and write. She grew up in Texas and South Louisiana and went to school at Millsaps College and Louisiana State University. Cynthia lives with her

husband and two young children in the Greater New Orleans Area, where they enjoy fishing and hand-line crabbing together.
www.cynthiaspoetry.com
Social Media:
https://www.facebook.com/cynthiaschaeferpoetry
https://www.instagram.com/cynthias.poetry

Eliana Vanessa is originally from Buenos Aires, Argentina. Her new Self-Published collection of poems, Life-Limbs (2022), is now available on Amazon. Also, the forthcoming chapbook, Break-Dancing With Worms, will be released
in April (2024).
She is @eliana_vanessa_1
on Instagram
Her website is www.elianavanessa.com

Carl Scharwath, has appeared globally with 150+ journals selecting his poetry, short stories, interviews, essays, plays or art photography. Two poetry books 'Journey To Become Forgotten' (Kind of a Hurricane Press).and 'Abandoned' (ScarsTv) have been published. Carl is the art editor for Minute Magazine, a dedicated runner and 2nd degree black-belt in Taekwondo. Carl Scharwath, has appeared globally with 150+ journals selecting his poetry, short stories, interviews, essays, plays or art photography. Two poetry books 'Journey To Become Forgotten' (Kind of a Hurricane Press).and 'Abandoned' (ScarsTv) have been published. Carl is the art editor for Minute Magazine, a dedicated runner and 2nd degree black- belt in Taekwondo.

Jeffrey Alfier's most recent book, *The Shadow Field*, was published by Louisiana Literature Journal & Press (2020). His lit journal credits include *The Carolina Quarterly*, *Copper Nickel*, *Emerson Review*, *Hotel Amerika*, *James Dickey Review*, *New York Quarterly*, and *Vassar Review*. He is co-editor of Blue Horse Pressand *San Pedro River Review*.

Gerardo Aristimuno, born in Argentina, moved to New Orleans along with his family in 1978 leaving behind a country in disarray under a military dictatorship. Avid reader and lover of language, he started

writing poetry and short stories at a young age.Gerardo has published "Prismas" a collection of Short stories and "Itinerarios" a Poetry Anthology, both in Spanish.
His poetry has been published in Literary Magazines from Puerto Rico, Argentina, Nicaragua and USA. Currently working on two novels.

Growing up in New Orleans shaped **Holly Woodie** and her words then off to New York City. Writing under the haze of lamplit streets and dark roofs, she honed her craft.
Holly Woodie has written since before time and says that getting back to playing keeps her awake, alive, and thriving. She remains grateful.

Afreda Hygh
Live and work in a world fond of freedom, utopia, and creativism. I am an unknown prophet who admires the silence of spiritual essence and the marvel of justified peace that is a beauty unrivaled. I am an educator whose philosophy is that life has the ability to proclaim its' profound wonders through the epiphany of speech and written words.

Chad Foret is a writer and editor from SE Louisiana and the author of Scenes from a Rain Country (Lavender Ink, 2022). Recent work appears or is forthcoming in Barrelhouse, storySouth, CutBank, Electric Literature, Prime Number Magazine, Bayou Magazine, Crab Creek Review, Barely South Review, and other journals and anthologies. More info can be found at chadforet.com.

Native New Orleanian **Dionne Charlet Baker** is a grandmother, poet, and former Renaissance festival Belle . Her poetry has been published online in such journals as *LadowichMagazine*, *Loose Words*, *A Cornered Gurl*, and *Assemblage* and anthologized in *The Poetry Buffet, An Anthology of New Orleans Poetry*, the *By Gaslight* Series, and the *Inklings: Louisiana Writers* Series.

Alton Paul Baker, Jr. (1/22/67 - 3/5/21) had just begun an inspired writing career chronicling his lifetime of dedication and love for Louisiana swampland. His handiwork can be viewed from the gates of the Algiers ferry dock to the ferry rails of the Chalmette boat, which he worked on as a deck hand with his mother. Al's words reflect the candor and gentle strength of spirit he boasted with a smile for all those graced to meet him.

Phillip T. Kehoe has spent over half his life in southern Louisiana with its rhythms, smells and tastes. He approaches his writing the same way he approaches his cooking, using whatever can be pulled out of his internal pantry, mixing and simmering and adjusting flavors until it is worthy to serve.
Time in south has made both his cooking and his writing both more nuanced and complex.

Ray Russell, pen name **Russell MacClaren**, has experience in most aspects of human endeavor: sports, scouting, military, construction, clergy and teaching.
He has three personal volumes of poetry and has edited for an on-line magazine. He has overseen workshops, read on TV and was seated on the board of two poetry societies. His poetry and short stories appear in numerous anthologies and on the net.

Gina Ferrara lives in New Orleans. She has several poetry collections including her latest, *Amiss*, published by Dos Madres Press in 2023. Since 2007, she has curated The Poetry Buffet, a monthly reading series held the first Saturday of each month. Her work has recently appeared in *Sixty Four Parishes, The Citron Review,* and *The Anacapa Review.*

www.ingramcontent.com/pod-product-compliance
Lightning Source LLC
LaVergne TN
LVHW010620100826
845148LV00014B/3052